NOT

FOR
SALE

FOR
PROMO
ONLY

NEW
DIRECTIONS
IN
PROMOTIONAL
DESIGN

Edited & Published by
Viction:ary

NOT
FOR
SALE
/
FOR
PROMO
ONLY

First published and distributed by
viction:workshop ltd.

viction:ary™

viction:workshop ltd.
Unit C, 7/F, Seabright Plaza, 9-23 Shell Street,
North Point, Hong Kong
Url: www.victionary.com   Email: we@victionary.com
www.facebook.com/victionworkshop

Edited and produced by viction:workshop ltd.

Concepts & art direction by Victor Cheung
Book design by viction:workshop ltd.

ISBN 978-988-17328-2-8
Printed and bound in China

NOT

FOR
SALE

FOR
PROMO
ONLY

NEW
DIRECTIONS
IN
PROMOTIONAL
DESIGN

Edited & Published by
Viction:ary

FORE WORD

BY
DEMIAN CONRAD
—
DEMIAN CONRAD
DESIGN

It has now been a few years that I contribute regularly to viction:ary activities and what I find astonishing is their sensitivity to synthesise and give back to us a great vision of the contemporary graphic design scene. It looks as if they are watching the world's production from a privilege skyscraper.

Promotion has always been a key point for all kinds of trade and cultural sharing. It empowers your idea, or your meme, and spreads it out as much as you can. In fact, I prefer to think in term of multiplication and variation. Living in a saturated market, it is really difficult for a brand to stand out, and even if you try to attract people by creating strange and different designs, like colouring a cow in purple as Seth Goldin said, it does not mean that you are going to hit the point or pass the deal. Personally, I strongly believe that a good promotion is based on the right setting of your communication and right choice of the values to share with your audience.

A good example, when I was approached by the Lausanne Underground Film and Movie Festival for the pitch, I had to make a clear statement which did underlined my qualities. During the meeting, when I was serving an Italian Mocha coffee, I also served three chocolate rabbits with their heads chopped off and laid down on the plate. Suddenly the committee started to laugh and connected with me. In that moment some important information passed, the understanding, the underground culture, the lateral thinking and the joy of life.

Promotion should be done on several levels, but more you resonate in values and pertinence to your audience, the more your will create a long term anchor.

This book is a great tool to understand better how people around the world connect in brilliant ways regarding and supporting their own culture. The beauty of promotions is in the desire to share our passions and our dreams.

There is an age old saying that 'you only get one chance to make a good impression'. That ideology may be short and sweet, but it truly is the best way to encompass everything within this book's pages. Creating an impact through visual design is something many of us do on a daily basis, communicating different messages to people we may never have met before, or who may never have heard of us before. From invitations to graduation shows, exhibitions and events, through to portfolios to postcards, they all share a few very important things in common. This first one is simple, any promotional piece must create a memorable impression. Most people are inundated daily with all kinds of communications, so it's crucial that your

FORE WORD

BY
MARK GRAHAM
—
ILOVEDUST

piece stands out from the crowd. However, creative design alone is only half the battle! In order to create maximum stand-out in a world saturated with promotional pieces, combining creative design with intelligent thinking is key to creating something that is truly memorable. So not only does it have to look amazing, for the information contained within to be retained, it must communicate a relevant message that resonates with its intended audience. And it's how you combine the two that's the tricky part!

Every promotional item has an 'expiry date', in that it can excite the market for one moment and vanish the next – as soon as something more exciting comes along to steal the limelight. So in order to

create a great promotional item, you need to ascertain just what it is that you need that item to tell people. It's almost irrelevant what your promotional piece is to be used for – the concept is fundamentally the same. Whether you are looking to attract new business, invite people to your design show, or raise awareness of you or your product – you must ensure you give people a good reason to do so. Include this within your piece and let the design do the talking. Show people why should they come and see your show, or try your new product, or work with you. And most importantly, show them what you do is different from your competitors. A great promotional piece will do this, because it addresses that very question before it's even been asked.

A good example of a great promotional piece that worked really well for us was the perfect fusion of great design and clever thinking. On our first trip to the Nike Campus in Portland, when we first started working with Nike, we wanted to take along something that would really stand out. So we produced 30 specially designed posters that featured the history of Portland, including memorable places within the city (thank you Google!) in the original ilovedust style. The posters got a great reception and when you walk around campus today, you can see a few of these framed in people's offices. People remember us just from that one screenprint, not just because it looked cool, but also because it was a well thought-out an idea that resonated with the people of Portland.

Original thinking - it works, it really does.

CONTRIBUTORS

& SMITH
A+B STUDIO
A2/SW/HK
AAD
ALEX TROCHUT
ALEXANDER LIS
ANGUS MACPHERSON
ARTIVA DESIGN
ASYLUM
B&W STUDIO
BLOW
CATALOGUE
CATARINA CARREIRAS
CLASEBCN
COLLECTIVE APPROACH
COMMANDO GROUP AS
COMMUNE
DEMIAN CONRAD DESIGN
DESIGNBOLAGET
DHNN (DESIGN HAS NO NAME)
DONNA WEARMOUTH
EVERYTHING DESIGN
GOODMORNING TECHNOLOGY
HAT-TRICK DESIGN
    CONSULTANTS LIMITED
HAWAII DESIGN
HELLO MONDAY

ILOVEDUST
JOHNSON BANKS
KANELLA
LLOYD & ASSOCIATES GMBH
MAGPIE STUDIO
MARC&ANNA
MARK BROOKS GRAPHIK DESIGN
MASH CREATIVE
MATTHEW HANCOCK
MELVILLE BRAND DESIGN
MIKA NASH
MIND DESIGN
MUTE
NB:STUDIO
NERVOUSWETHANDS
NOOKA INC.
NOUS VOUS
OSCAR DIAZ STUDIO
PAPERLUX GMBH
PLOTZ
REKLAM2010, BECKMANS COLLEGE
    OF DESIGN
RESEARCH AND DEVELOPMENT
ROANDCO, THE COMPANY &
    COLLABORATIONS OF
    ROANNE ADAMS
ROB SCHELLENBERG

RUIZ+COMPANY
SAMANTHA ZIINO
SEBASTIEN LORDEZ
SEESAW DESIGN
SMEL
STUDIO LIN
STUDIO ROUND
STUDIOMAKGILL
SUSANNE DUNKEL
THREE & CO.
TOKYO PISTOL CO., LTD.
TOUCH BRANDING
TURNSTYLE
UNDERLINE STUDIO
VBG
WATARU YOSHIDA
ZOO STUDIO S.L.

INDEX

 DIRECT MARKETING
If skillfully crafted, direct mailers would be more than just a fact sheet. Through creative and art directions, not only do these ads introduce noteworthy features of new products, but also inspire needs, desires and arouse interest in a certain topic that customers could hardly imagine or realise on their own.

 SELF PROMOTION
Self-promotional items are literally a designer's CV. Naturally expected to represent one's competence to produce visually powerful and effective designs, it takes a designer's every single resources to create the maximum impact, something remarkable and appealing out of a limited budget before they get any deal.

 BRAND COMMUNICATIONS
Every business requires a brand. It is what a consumer needs to identify a service provider among the many; and how business positions itself. From corporate stationery to brand books and annual reports, the approaches aim to communicate visions, make promises and parallel beliefs from multiple aspects.

 SEASONAL GREETINGS
Can something undesirable be regarded as a thoughtful gift? Sent out as an expression of gratitude or regards, seasonal greetings are definitely something more than a freebie or some anonymous surprises that expects nothing in return. Regardless, it is a lighthearted way to re-connect to your clients.

 EVENT CAMPAIGNS
Created mostly for one-off functions, event identities and announcements immerse recipients into the atmosphere prior to their presence in the event. Vivid and informative, they explain the values of being a part and raise awareness of what is happening in town. But most vital of all, they intrigue and draw attention.

SWEATING TEASER

➤■ Sweating teaser came as Nervouswethands started building up his name when he stepped into the business world of design. The name of the practice was thought to be the designers' best representation, for the tense and passion that underlaid his creations. It was somehow one of his favourite ideas of sending something similar to serial killer clues, which also bore clear reference to the practice's name. Inside the pack were two gloves with which he used to draw, a card and some other else. ■■◤

⊙ *Design: Nervouswethands*

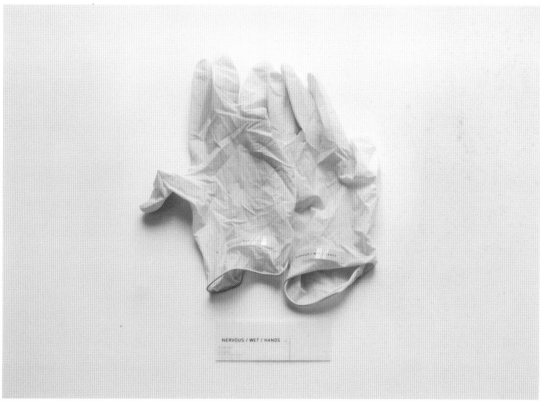

NERVOUS / WET / HANDS

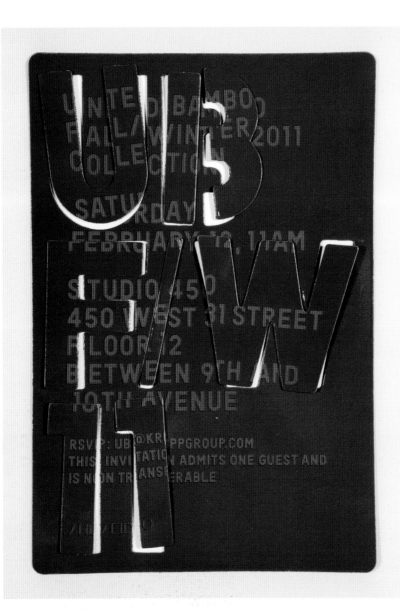

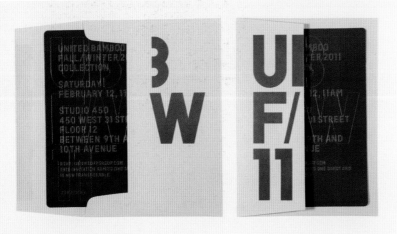

UB INVITATIONS

▶■ The invitations to United Bamboo's fashion shows in 2011 challenged Studio Lin's inventiveness within the frame of a standard size envelope and tight budget. The results were two durable solutions that make references to respective seasonal themes. Designed for United Bamboo's spring/summer collection was an iron-on badge with shiny embroidered types and a blue colour scheme reminiscent of a bright day on the ocean. For the fall/winter show was a piece of magnet inspired by the collection's mod and androgynous motif. ■■◀

⊙ Design: Studio Lin // Client: United Bamboo

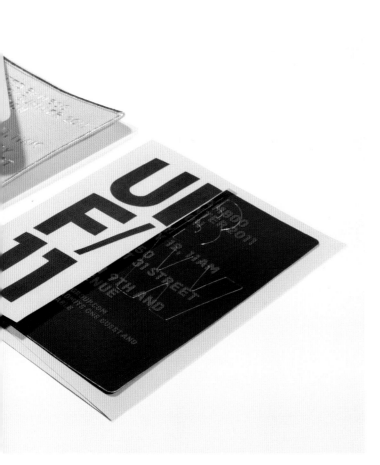

**UNITED BAMBOO
SPRING/SUMMER 2011
COLLECTION**

**SATURDAY
SEPTEMBER 11, 11AM**

**HOSFELT GALLERY
531 WEST 36 STREET
BETWEEN 10TH AND
11TH AVENUE**

RSVP: UBRSVP@KRUPPGROUP.COM
THIS INVITATION ADMITS ONE GUEST AND
IS NON TRANSFERABLE

SHISEIDO

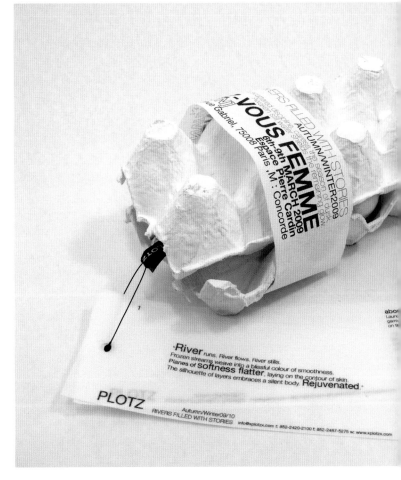

 # PARIS A/W 2009

▶■ PLOTZ's 2009 A/W collection was about a sensuous stimulation aroused by the unsettled motion in the apparently quiet river with a little poetic sense. Inspired by the theme, River Filled with Stories, PLOTZ assembled a complex, composed of a USB drive and a pen, as an gift pack given out at fashion fair, Rendez-Vous Femme, held in Paris. Using an egg carton to hold the items in place, the pack was also bound and tagged with strips, explaining the stories behind the collection and the brand itself. ■◀

◉ Design: PLOTZ

been pertaining to the spirit of communication between
already reached the public, PLOTZ has made an impact
front of style while sticking to their own characters.

ty of styles, PLOTZ stressed details from garments to
they are uncovered through collections. PLOTZ
ome details provide comforts and
or relief.

er 09/10 Collection, entitled « RIVERS FILLED
RIES », A sensuous stimulation aroused by the
in the apparently quiet river, a series of carefully
ns which transforms the subtle torrent in the flow into a
arments, creating a delicate yet complicated elegance on

ollection, PLOTZ continues its experiment with fragile fabric in
ms and patterns. Silk and chiffon are draped and pleated into
looking folds that resemble the flowing currents. A black strap
op to bottom delivers a twisted styling. Alongside the colours of
he tonal change of black and grey is contrasted with dark orange.
ult is a fluidity with enhanced volume veiling across the body
it visually interesting and romantic.

of this new series of ready-to-wear shows some more maturity in
's tailoring and hts novel infusion of a solitary romance.

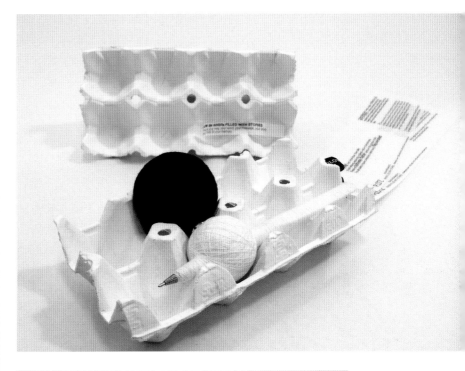

AIGA SEATTLE
PARTY INVITATION

▶■■ AIGA Seattle's membership party was planned to take place in Space Needle, a major landmark in the city. Specially requested to highlight the venue, Turnstyle was serendipitously surprised by the potential to reconfigure the letterforms of "AIGA" into an approximation of the space needle. Featuring four enormous letters with detail instructions, the invitation asked recipients to build their own Space Needle that can stand aside as a lively reminder on the desk. ■■◀

◉ *Design: Turnstyle // Client: AIGA Seattle*

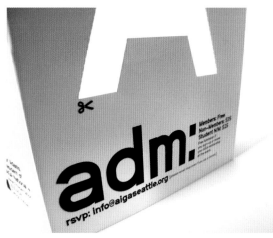

SONY ERICSSON XPERIA PURENESS INVITATION

▶■ Pureness was Sony Ericsson's latest mobile phone had been reduced to just the essentials, allowing users to do nothing more than talk, messaging and time checks. To give the media a heads-up about the minimal nature of the new handy that also carried a transparency feature, Melville hyped the press event with an acrylic glass invitation. The graphic appearance corresponded the idea with Black Helvetica. Rather less, but good. Just like the new Pureness. ■◄

⊙ *Design: Melville Brand Design // Client: Häberlein & Mauerer (PR Agency), Sony Ericsson*

BLACK & WHITE CHRISTMAS

▶■ Aiming for publicity, new contacts and opportunities, Matthew Hancock started the piece with a great deal of experimentation and research into the iconography of Christmas. It became very complex at one point, before it was refined down to the extremely simple end product. The cards were foil blocked in white onto high quality black stock. They were mailed out with no further information, so as to provoke curiosity and generate traffic on his portfolio on the net. ■■◀

◉ *Design: Matthew Hancock // Special Credit: Benwells, London*

M&A

◀■ MARC&ANNA is a graphic design consultancy founded by Marc Atkinson and Anna Ekelund. Emphasising "duality", the ampersand sign centred the design in various styles. Examples of successful pairs, such as Gin&Tonic or Bubble&Squeak, were also listed in the direct mail poster, with the strapline "Some combinations just work". Reversible letterheads were purposed so sensible letters could be sent out with the name, MARC&ANNA or, alternatively, Bangers&Mash, on the front. ■■◀

⊙ Design: MARC&ANNA

BUBBLE SQUEAK
GIN TONIC
R B
TOM JERRY
TRINIDAD TOBAGO
JEANS TRAINERS
SENSE SENSIBILITY
BANGERS MASH
BACON EGG
ASTERIX OBELIX
EAST END BOYS WEST END GIRLS
BED BREAKFAST
CUT PASTE
M M'S
NUTS BOLTS
FOOLS HORSES
SALT VINEGAR
THE OWL THE PUSSYCAT
SKULL CROSSBONES
TERMS CONDITIONS
STARSKY HUTCH
MARC & ANNA

BUBBLE

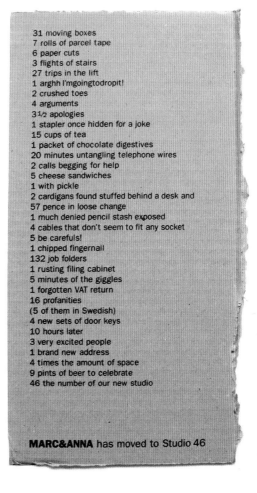

31 moving boxes
7 rolls of parcel tape
6 paper cuts
3 flights of stairs
27 trips in the lift
1 arghh I'mgoingtodropit!
2 crushed toes
4 arguments
3½ apologies
1 stapler once hidden for a joke
15 cups of tea
1 packet of chocolate digestives
20 minutes untangling telephone wires
2 calls begging for help
5 cheese sandwiches
1 with pickle
2 cardigans found stuffed behind a desk and
57 pence in loose change
1 much denied pencil stash exposed
4 cables that don't seem to fit any socket
5 be carefuls!
1 chipped fingernail
132 job folders
1 rusting filing cabinet
5 minutes of the giggles
1 forgotten VAT return
16 profanities
(5 of them in Swedish)
4 new sets of door keys
10 hours later
3 very excited people
1 brand new address
4 times the amount of space
9 pints of beer to celebrate
46 the number of our new studio

MARC&ANNA has moved to Studio 46

MOVING CARD

Having moved into a brand spanking new studio, the duo wanted to notify everyone of the news and excitement, especially the clients of MARC&ANNA. A list of relevant numbers about the relocation was screenprinted onto the flaps of some used cardboard moving boxes, on top of the central message – an updated address. The mailers were said to have baffled the British postmen before they reached their clients' hands. ■■◀

◉ *Design: MARC&ANNA*

 1+1=3

▶■■ "One plus one becomes three" illustrates how new ideas always come into sight when two persons meet. Taken as the theme of Stockholm Furniture Fair, where Form2009, a group of 11 product design third-year students from Beckmans College of Design would attend and introduce their work, R10 took the job to promote the event by materialising the idea with the entire showcase. R10 was a group of second-year students in advertising and graphic design from the same college, including Petter Prinz, Kalle Hagman, Andreas Lewandowski, John Falk Rodén, Linn Mork, Samuel Nilsson and Martin Wågnert. ■■◀

⊙ *Design: Reklam2010 (R10)* // *Client: Form2009*

KARIN WIDMARK

GABRIELLA MATHENY

HELENA SVENSSON

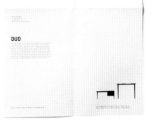

"
STEEL
—
HARD
HEAVY
AND
DEAD
"

DUO

"
IT
COULD
BE
AN
OCTOPUS
AND
YOU
THE
FISHERMAN
"

COLLAPSIBLE
STOOL

"
JUST
FUN TO
PLAY
WITH
"

MOVE
ON
UP

 # HOMMAGE À KOSUTH

▶■■ Offering a different angle to look at Demian Conrad, the designer, and his creative directions, the setting for photo shoot was also a tribute to Joseph Kosuth, an American artist known for his conceptual art pieces, but with Conrad's little possessions taking over the space. Photographed and printed into posters and postcards, the whole assemble represents Conrad's three core disciplines - idea creation, product design and graphic design. ■■◤

◉ Design: DEMIAN CONRAD DESIGN // Photography: YUNA MATHIEU-CHOVET

WARM REGARDS

Short for "Art and Design", Aad is a Dublin-based design studio with its roots in graphic design. For them design is about crafting thought, idea and strategy, art and the visual language they would use to engage and communicate. Expressing "warm regards" by sending out a piece of scarf at Christmas time was how Aad put words to work. Dublin clothing label, ARMS, was the maker of the garment delivered in a card packaging a die-cut "warm regards" on the outside. ■■◤

⊙ *Design: Aad*

Warm
Regards
From
Aad

In order to deliver our
warmest of regards we've
commissioned a limited
edition scarf from
Dublin's brightest new
clothing label – Arms /
www.aadfromdublin.com

Here's to your christmas
being as warm as your
new scarf

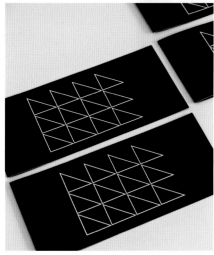

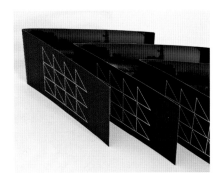

 # BRASIL ARQUITETURA

◗■ Brasil Arquitetura was a reappraisal of a Brazilian architectural practice's achievements in furniture and exhibition design led by its founders Francisco Fanucci and Marcelo Carvalho Ferraz. Given a month to deliver a promotional suite for the event, ARTIVA started developing a synthetic image, a modular shape, to be the compelling visual to represent the architectural process and idea on multiple applications, with a few given pictures in hand. The shape was also extended to inform the idea on the promotional cards, posters, info graphics for the exhibition. ■■◤

◉ *Design: ARTIVA DESIGN // Client: Casartarc*

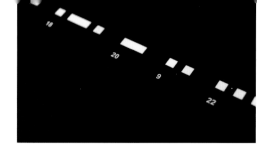

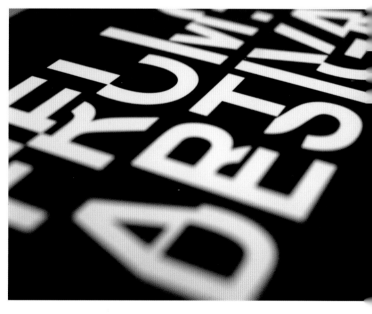

HELLO FROM ARTIVA

A stack of minimal postcards was printed to pass on a simple message, Hello from ARTIVA, for anyone who might not be aware of the name. The morse code image was the most curious idea of the card, a visual translation of a "banal phrase" instead of the more commonly-read or decipherable words. ARTIVA was taking this simple and cost-effective pieces to promote their studies on graphics and visuals. The cards were left in strategic places such as bookshops of museums and exhibition spaces.

◉ *Design: ARTIVA DESIGN*

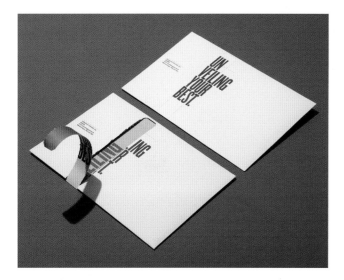

NUARS — UNVEILING YOUR BEST

▶■ NUARs is an annual national competition held by Unisource, a major distributor of paper and graphic arts supplies in Canada, to acknowledge the excellence in print production and design. With the spirit laid in creative presentation, Underline came up with the theme, "Unveiling Your Best", and actualised the idea through flat graphics and designs. Elements included photographing a two-layer paper craft for the poster and a custom peel-off design on the invitation envelopes. ■◀

◉ *Design: Underline Studio // Client: Unisource Canada // Photography: Shanghoon // Printing: Annan & Sons*

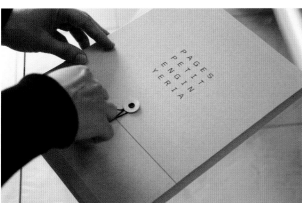

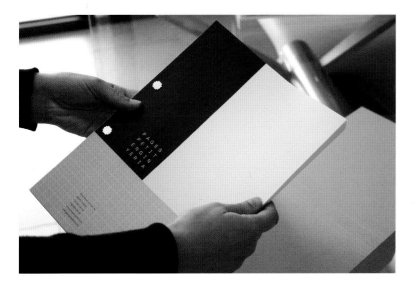

PAGESPETIT

With Pagespetit Enginyeria newly introduced to the world of industrial engineering, the goal of this corporate image project was to find the correct elements that could magnify the contrast between a high-tech engineering project and craftsmanship, and understand the things in between. The paper project folder came as a perfect solution that could also well-define the values of the brand. The delicate artisan style folder was used to envelop and deliver project ideas and plans, in an organised and exquisite way.

Design: Zoo Studio S.L. // Client: Pagespetit Enginyeria

 # SIX SITES FOR SOUND

▶■■ The job was about designing a catalogue with attachments for a sound art exhibition held in six different locations. It became an enjoyable but complicated project for Mind Design as they had trouble finding rubber bands to match the width of the attached CD on a relatively small budget. The catalogue and the CD were eventually held together by two custommade rubber bands with the speaker icon and title, inspired by the volume scales on old stereo systems, stamped on by hand. ■■◤

◉ *Design: Mind Design // Client: Resonance FM*

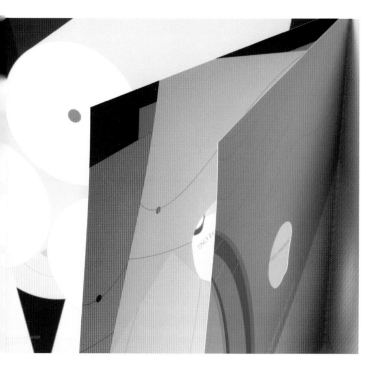

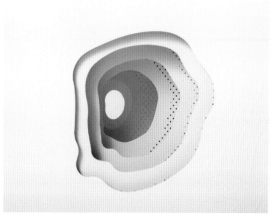

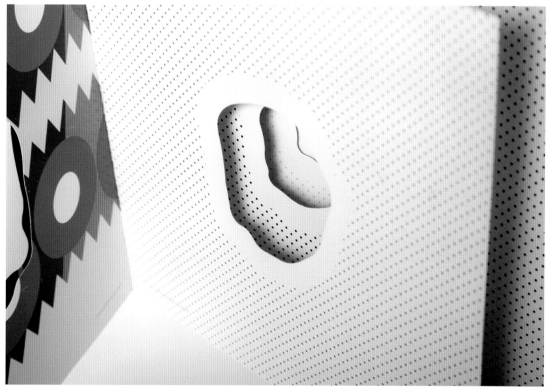

♟ D2 RECYCLED
❋ PRINT BROCHURE

▶■ From the forest where trees as the raw material were grown, through to the pulp mill, paper mill to paper merchant, and finally a finished paper product – the journey of paper-making, revealed in a combination of layers, cutouts, illustrations and graphics demonstrated how environmentally conscious D2 was while they produce prints. The piece was composed to manifest their FSC accreditation and their environmental awareness within their industry. ■◀

◉ *Design: ilovedust // Client: D2 Printer*

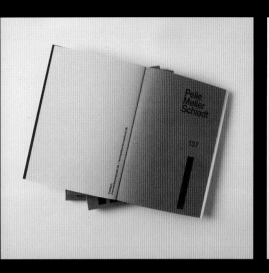

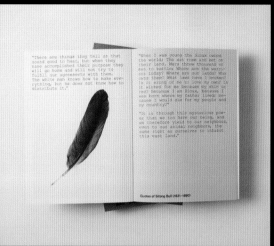

♜ FUNEN ART ACADEMY
♜ GRADUATION CATALOGUE

▶■■ The Funen Art Academy wanted a catalogue and thereby a visual identity for their graduate's and graduation show. Eleven emerging artists would take part in the exhibition but each in an independent style. A countdown sign, with five strokes in a pack, typical on the walls of jail in movies, was used to imply the final moments these students had left in the institution, as well as the number of graduates in the show. Each student was dedicated to a colour, revealed at the spine of the catalogue book. ■■◀

◉ *Design: Designbolaget // Client: The Funen Art Academy*

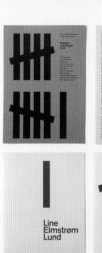

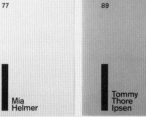

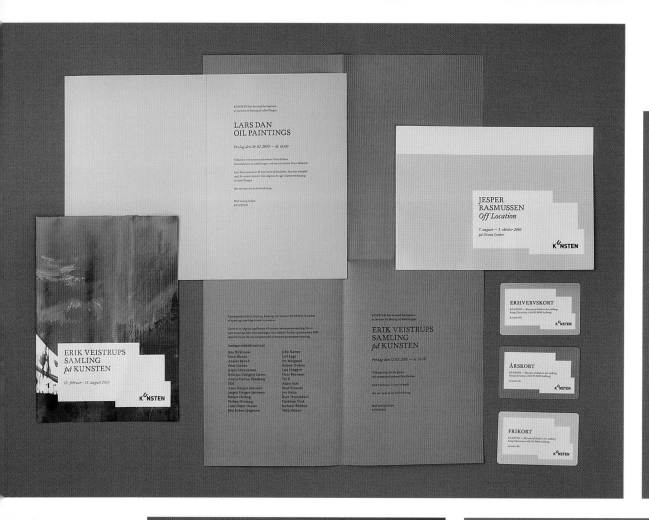

KUNSTEN MUSEUM OF MODERN ART AALBORG VISUAL IDENTITY

KUNSTEN Museum of Modern Art Aalborg is unique in both its architectural design and art collection. Constructed in the 1960s, the museum is prominent for its flexible layout permitted by its mobile partition walls and unique use of natural light, designed by famous Finnish architect, Alvar Aalto. The museum wanted a stronger identity, including a corporate palette, to strengthen its brand image. The logo abstractly depicts the signature outline of the building that is recognisable with or without text, on art or stand alone.

Design: Designbolaget // Client: KUNSTEN Museum of Modern Art Aalborg

 BASSMENT

▰▰ Bassment is a DJ collective based in York, where young professionals should go and chill in live jazz music and a glass of drink in hand. One of the proposals Angus Macpherson and Phil Armson had for Bassment was a set of eye catching and high impact identity products that lent little visual reference to the music genre and culture itself. The logo design offered a range of flexible extensions as poster graphics, flyers, beer mats, as well as record sleeves illustrations. ▰▰◄

⊙ Design: Angus MacPherson, Phil Armson // Client: Bassment

 QUIZ PARTY INVITATION

Printing company Gavin Martin Associates was planning a pub quiz evening to thank their clients. Making references to the informality and venue of the event, a set of eight invitations was produced, with inspiration from the rich visual heritage of beer mat design. Varied in shapes and colours, each mat featured a catchphrase alluding to the company's attribute or a member of staff. Details of the annual party were handwritten on the reverse, like the way bar patrons take beer mats as handy notepads.

⊙ *Design: & SMITH // Client: Gavin Martin Associates*

 ## EVERYTHING XMAS BEER

▶■ Everything has already established a protocol for their promotions and communications with messages built around their name "Everything". For Christmas in 2010, the Auckland-based practice's gift for their clients was a piece of sincere advice. Labelled 'Everything in moderation', Everything wished their clients a merry but responsible Christmas with half a dozen beers, demonstrating the six phrases of how Santa started celebrating Christmas with a little tipple and ended up in a bit of a mess. ■■◀

⊙ Design: Everything Design // Photography: Sandii McDonald

PAPER SCISSOR STONE TOTE BAGS

▰▰ Paper Scissor Stone is a chic boutique launched to bring art and fashion together through their handpicked fashion offerings sourced or designed by the founders from around the world. Picturing its name in three classic Mickey-styled hands, the tote bag print turned the shop's shopping bag into an accessory and a "walking ad" as the customers feel happy to reuse the bag. Bags were given away as customers made a purchase at the store. ▰▰◀

◉ *Design: Catalogue // Client: Paper Scissor Stone*

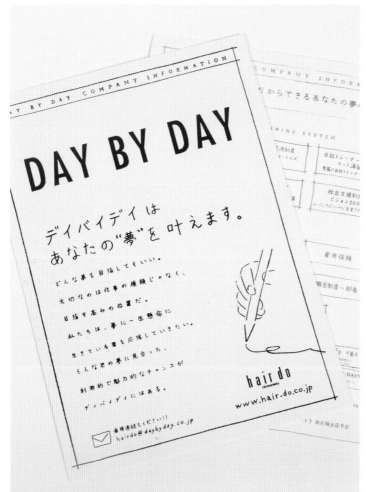

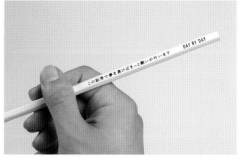

DAY BY DAY
PROMOTION TOOL

▶■■ DAY BY DAY is a hair salon with an objective to "value every dream". To reinforce that belief among its students who were about to graduate school, a stationery set was handed out so each of them could write down their dreams and promises to pursuit their profession with their heart and soul. The set was composed of a card and pencil with words of encouragement and faith. ■■◀

◉ Design: TOKYO PISTOL CO., LTD. // Client: DAY BY DAY / SEYFERT

THE WORKS EXHIBITION 2011 INVITATION

It is usually the creativity and originality in the invitation design that would draw a promising response to the graduate exhibition of Communication Design Honours projects. With a geometric theme, Samantha Ziino constructed an origami-envelope pack with a pastel ink stamp to reveal a unique print pattern when unfolded. A thousand invitations were printed and distributed to the public, families and other fellow students. The geometric pattern were also rolled out into the graduate catalogue and became the identity for the year.

Design: Samantha Ziino // Client: RMIT University // Special Credit: Stephanie Pellas

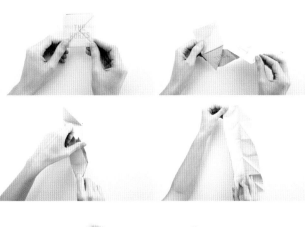

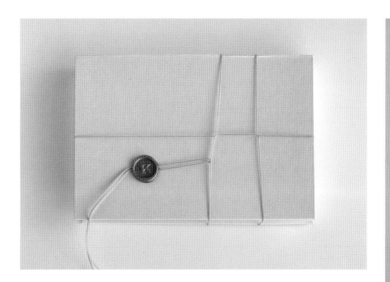

☷ YELLOW THREAD

 "Yellow thread" was Kanella's yet-another smart, discreet promotional package made based on a personal belief – DESIGN is the KEY to the PATH towards the SUN. The project was inspired by the story of Ariadne, a Greek myth character, and her thread, with a goal to praise design in physical materials. The set contained four recycled carton cards with the studio's iconic dots embossed to compose a couple of blind illustrations under the hand-sewed words. ■■◣

◉ *Design: Kanella*

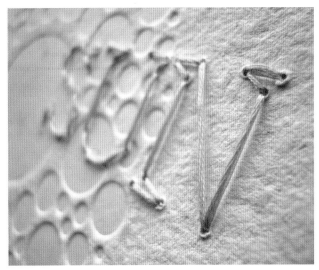

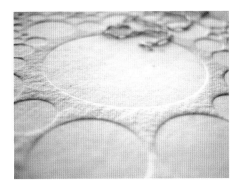

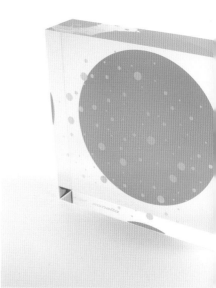

✦ DAY AND NIGHT

▶▬ Coming in two versions, thick plexi-glass and thick cardboard, DAY and NIGHT was another round of limited self-promotional packages by Kanella, based around the studio's signature circles and dots. That concept of "Simple can be beautiful when it lays on a strong idea" was vital in her work. The spots form an interactive element and element of surprise as they capture light in the day and reveal a circle of glowing stars in the dark. ▬◀

⊙ *Design: Kanella*

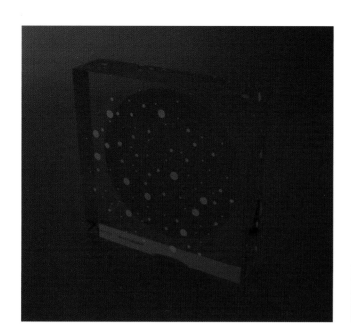

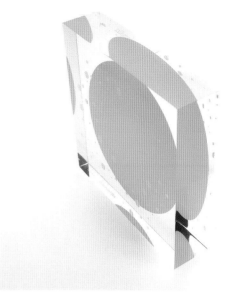

Day and night

An object that captures the day's sun
and at night reveals a cluster of stars
that glow in the dark.

May this ray of light mesmerize
your senses and brighten up your world.

Limited edition 0/20

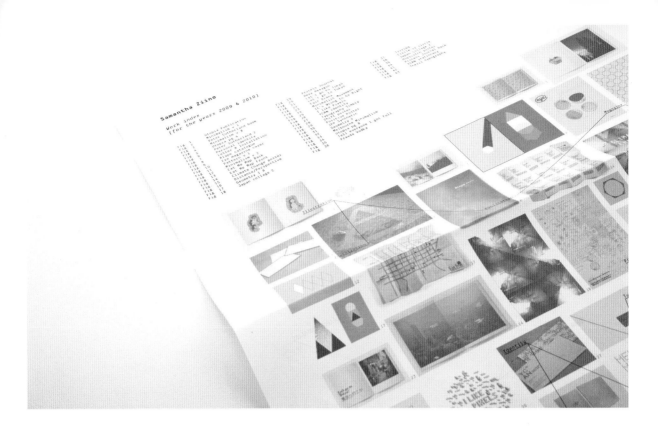

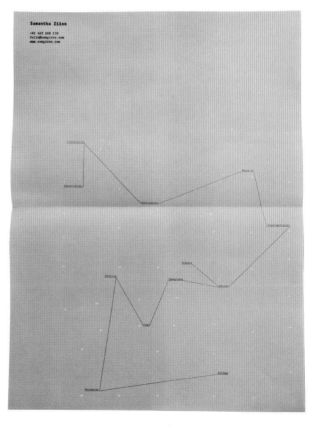

WORK INDEX

▶■ Recently graduated with a wide-ranging portfolio of graphic projects and photography work to represent herself, Samantha Ziino would require a mailer-poster to promote her work and herself. Aiming for a collective representation rather than specific highlights, projects of variant disciplines were spread out in reduced colours and size of thumbnails to introduce a portfolio with greater details on the designer's website. Images were linked up with a line path to connect and specify areas of design. ■◀

⊙ *Design: Samantha Ziino*

JPP SYNTHETIC

KW Doggett Paper was going to introduce a new synthetic paper line, which was very durable, food safe and water resistant. Three paper models were constructed and photographed to symbolically highlight the unique qualities of the new product named JPP. The design contained two parts, three double-sided loose cards and a poster with the key features and names of product and supplier, i.e. KW Doggett, repeatedly appearing on different parts of the collateral. The package was intended for designer clients of KW Doggett.

⊙ *Design: Samantha Ziino // Client: KW Doggett Paper*

♛ SONY ERICSSON
♦ PRESS INVITATION

▷■■ Sony Ericsson was about to hold a press event in Stockholm. Part of this campaign was to ask a group of German lifestyle journalists to organise a trip to Stockholm, with the essential features of the brand's phones compared with elements of earth, water, fire and air. Melville created a playful "elementary" mix for the invitation, with a teaser, invitation and an individualised map of Stockholm. A hand-folded heaven-and-earth game was attached to add a fun element in the package. ■■◀

◉ *Design: Melville Brand Design // Client: Häberlein & Mauerer (Agency), Sony Ericsson*

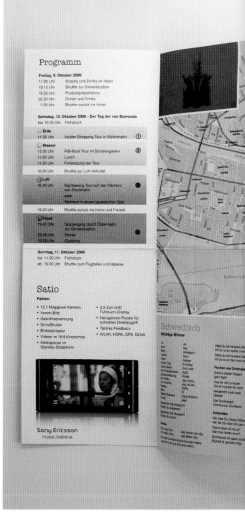

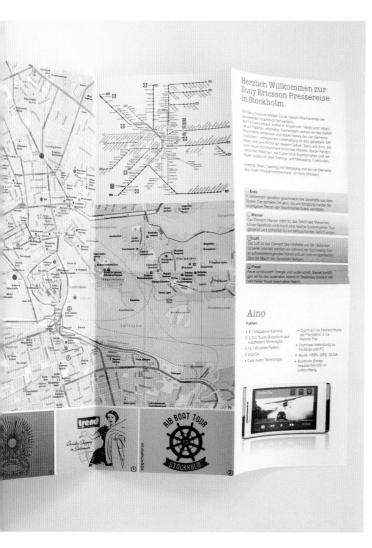

Herzlich Willkommen zur
Sony Ericsson Pressereise
in Stockholm.

Mit Sony Ericsson erlebst Du an diesem Wochenende die
pulsierende Hauptstadt Schwedens.
Auf 14 Inseln erbaut, treffen in Stockholm Trends und Urbani-
tät auf Tradition und Natur. Gemeinsam werden wir die Vielfalt
Stockholms entdecken und dabei keines der vier Elemente
auslassen – unbegrenzte Unterhaltung ist also garantiert. Mit
Satio und zwei Profis auf diesem Gebiet, Satio und Aino, die
zwei neuen Entertainment Unlimited-Modelle. Beide Handys
verbinden Walkman- mit Cyber-shot-Eigenschaften und ver-
fügen zusätzlich über Gaming- und Messaging-Funktionen.

Imaging, Music, Gaming und Messaging sind die vier Elemente
des neuen Produktversprechens von Sony Ericsson.

Erde
In Södermalm sprießen geschmackvolle Geschäfte aus dem
Boden. Der perfekte Ort also, wo uns Shopping-Insider die
wichtigsten Trends der Stockholmer Szene vermitteln.

Wasser
Das Element Wasser steht für das Gefühl des Menschen.
Unser Spieltrieb wird durch eine rasante Schärengarten-Tour
geweckt und sicherlich für ein berauschendes Gefühl sorgen.

Luft
Die Luft ist das Element des Intellekts und der Gedanken.
Unseren Intellekt werden wir während der Sightseeing-Tour
in schwindelerregenden Höhen schulen oder im spaßhaften
Sinn die Macht der Gedanken festigen.

Feuer
Feuer symbolisiert Energie und Leidenschaft. Beides benöti-
gen sie für den lodernden Abend im Steakhaus sowie in der
von heißer Musik beschallten Nacht.

Aino

Fakten:

- 8.1 Megapixel-Kamera
- 3-Zoll Touch-Bildschirm aus kratzfestem Mineralglas
- 16.7 Millionen Farben
- WQVGA
- Clear Audio Technologie

- Zugriff auf die Medieninhalte der Playstation 3 via Remote Play
- Drahtlose Verbindung zu Media.Go und PC
- WLAN, HSPA, GPS, DLNA
- Bluetooth Stereo Headset MH100 im Lieferumfang

BABYLON GARDENS IDENTITY

 Babylon Gardens is a landscape design and construction start-up owned by a young and dynamic husband-and-wife team. What gardening is to Babylon is what food is to Jamie Oliver – they are passionate about creating a peaceful sanctuary for young families in New Zealand using only natural and low-VOC products with preference for local suppliers. Everything's branding and marketing strategies for the company were set out to reflect just that, with warmth and energy fueling the practice's website and communications. ■◄

◉ *Design: Everything Design // Client: Babylon Gardens // Photography: Sandii McDonald*

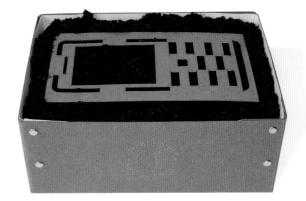

 # HAVE A GREEN HEART

▰▰ Sony Ericsson had developed an environmentally-friendly phone that required less power than normal phones to operate. To draw the media's attention to the new product and the brand's sustainability programme, Melville created a sustainable mailing with only recycled materials to use among the cotton soil bag, seed packet, cardboard container and the paper cast of the phone. The emphatic part was that recipients could grow and eat their own cress plant with the tools provided. ▰▰◀

◉ *Design: Melville Brand Design // Client: Häberlein & Mauerer (PR Agency), Sony Ericsson*

 # MIT MUSEUM
– EXHIBITION
IDENTITY

▶■■ Museum of Modern Art Aalborg was planning an exhibition, Mit Museum, as an innovative approach to initiate a two-way dialogue and engage visitors with the museum itself. The graphics made for the exhibition had a bit of an anarchistic approach, with a titled logo and line striking through the text, to encourage creative interpretations over the informality. Tape rolls were also handed out so visitors could frame whatever they would define as art. ■■◀

◉ *Design: Designbolaget // Client: KUNSTEN Museum of Modern Art Aalborg*

 # NIT MANGA 5 CAMPAIGN

▶▬ Japanzone is a Catalan portal founded on the enthusiasm for Asian cinema, manga, animation and Japanese culture. Nit Manga is one of its cultural events dedicated to manga fans. To draw maximum attention for the night, Zoo created two sets of posters and flyers to give away in shops and bars. Each set contains a collection of four character faces in fluorescent colours with a hint of variety and richness in the manga culture. ▬◀

⊙ *Design: Zoo Studio S.L. // Client: Japanzone*

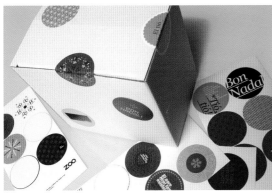

 # GIFT FOR CHRISTMAS

A stack of sticker pads was sent off as a Christmas surprise for Zoo's clients. Printed with patterns, wit and Zoo's key value and creative, the stickers were intended to be the seeds of joy to pass on as recipients use them to decorate their own Christmas gifts. It was an entertaining process for the creative too, as they mix traditional Christmas phrases and concepts with a modern approach. ■■◀

⦿ Design: Zoo Studio S.L.

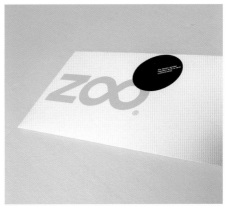

 # INSTABLE

▶▬▬ Instable is a community of talented photographers and recent graduates from the CEPV ESAA de Vevey. For the very first time they came together to exhibit their photography work, an identity system was constructed to highlight the individuality of the 12 participating artists, as well as the event as a whole. A set of patterns were drawn and applied across the event's posters, invitations and environment, interacting with each other to represent the kind of diversity on display. The campaign targeted curators, photographers, artists and students. ▬▬◀

◉ *Design: DEMIAN CONRAD DESIGN // Client: Collectif de photographes Instables*

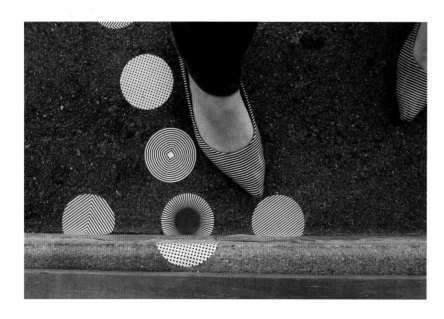

 # NIPPON CONNECTION 2011

➤■■ The Nippon Connection Japanese film festival is a gathering place for Japanese movie lovers, film makers and artists in Frankfurt, but the year 2011 also represented 150 years of German-Japanese friendship and a tough time for Japanese after the devastating tsunami struck their country. Using only pink and brown, visuals were stripped down to a plain yet flexible vector poster that could be easily recognised in its many variations. The folds made for a subtle clue of Japanese origami art. ■■◀

⊙ *Design: Alexander Lis, Katja Baumann, Lorenz Klingebiel // Client: Nippon Connection e.V*

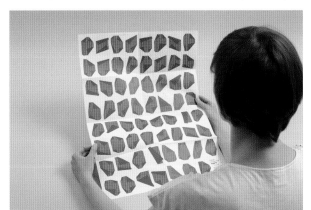

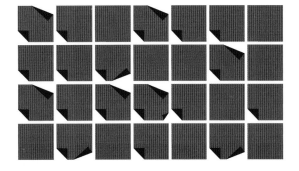

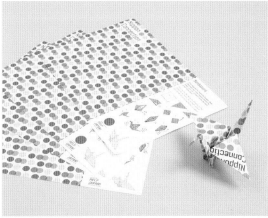

 # NIPPON CONNECTION 2010

The year 2010 was a celebratory mark for introducing Japanese movies to movie lovers, film makers and artists in Frankfurt. For the tenth Nippon Connection, a poster collection was specially produced to give cinema-goers a brief revision of the classics that have been featured in the festival over the decade. Each poster was a vivid interpretation of the titles connected with a strong type and pink theme.

Design: Alexander Lis, Catrin Altenbrandt, Catrin Sonnabend, Adrian Niessler, Kai Bergmann // Client: Nippon Connection e.V

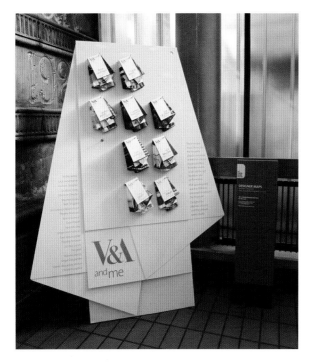

V&A MAPS

Victoria & Albert Museum was the hub of London Design Festival 2010. During the nine-day event, the museum had lent space for an array of specially commissioned installations and a broad programme of special events, talks and workshops for visitors to enjoy. Stemmed from a discussion about designers' inspirations and V&A's influences, ten A2 sized maps were produced to map a distribution of designers, authors and media figures. Each map were specially folded and hung from a stand alluding to the unique folds. ■■◀

◉ Design: johnson banks, Bethan Jones // Client: V&A Museum // Photography: Leon Steele, Tal Silverman // Model & Stand construction: Wesley West

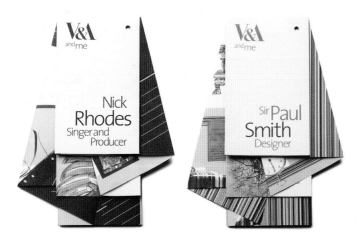

COLLECTIVE APPROACH
PROMOTIONAL MAILER

▶■ Having retrieved a large collection of antique London postcards, Collective Approach decided to give them a new lease of life and send them out once more as a promotional mailer for the studio. Completely unique with postage stamps and handwriting that dated back as early as 1901, each postcard were mounted on a cardboard and over-printed with the collective's expertise. The piece of promotional work were sent to touch base with studio clients and drive traffic to the company's website. ■◀

⊙ *Design: Collective Approach*

Synergy

Integrity

Dedication

Innovation

Hard Work

Humanity

BrandScents™
Be Different. Smell Different.

Does your brand stink?

Let's say you have a choice between two supermodels. Both are incredibly gorgeous, sophisticated and loaded with cash. Which one will you choose? The one that smells like your brother's reclusive uncle or the one that smells like diamonds? Logos and corporate colors only have a brief moment to make an impression, while brand odor can linger much longer. Negative odor can spoil brand equity, souring consumer opinion. If left unmanaged, brands can turn rancid.

Introducing:

Does your brand stink?

Let's say you have a choice between two supermodels. Both are incredibly gorgeous, sophisticated and loaded with cash. Which one will you choose? The one that smells like your brother's reclusive uncle or the one that smells like diamonds? Logos and corporate colors only have a brief moment to make an impression, while brand odor can linger much longer. Negative odor can spoil brand equity, souring consumer opinion. If left unmanaged, brands can turn rancid.

Introducing:

 BRANDSCENTS

➤▬ Does your brand stink? Is innovation in the air? These are the questions Turnstyle asked when they were trying to put ideas together to sell BrandScents. With BrandScents set up to help companies establish a pervasive brand presence, the team compared the brand with air fresheners capable of producing a subtle brand impression that would linger without being overbearing. Recipients of the direct mailer were invited to unseal the mailer and unlock a smell symbolic of inappropriate brand strategies that would better be replaced. ▬▬◄

◉ Design: Turnstyle

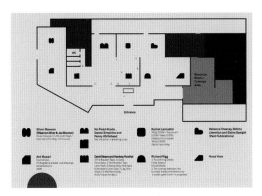

MORPHIC RESONANCE

Morphic Resonance was an experimental project where artists and artist collectives were invited to use Project Space Leeds, an independent art space, as an extended studio space to work and exhibit the results. As one of the participating artists, Nous Vous created a poster and graphic system that could perform to represent individuals as well as the project as a whole. The final solution featured an over-arching language where individual artists could own a shape and use it however they saw fit. ■■◀

◉ *Design: Nous Vous // Client: Project Space Leeds (PSL)*

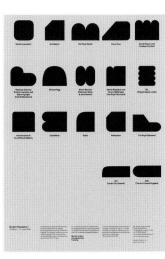

 EFTA

Set up to establish agreements between countries for the exchange of goods and people, the European Free Trade Association (EFTA) has been a key institution for Switzerland as an exporting country. While the Swiss Post planned to issue a special stamp to commemorate its 50th anniversary, Demain Conrad adopted a constructivist style to transmit the institute's values of liability, stability and solidity. The idea of cross-border trading was also conveyed as the anagram moves from one side of the perforations to another, like the customs of a country. ■■◄

◉ Design: DEMIAN CONRAD DESIGN // Client: Swiss Post // Photography: Sylvain Meltz

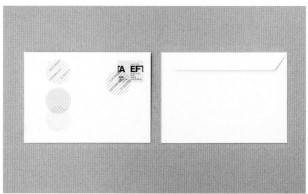

SEND A LETTER

V&A Village fete has been held annually to put an alternative spin on the British Design Scene at Victoria and Albert Museum in London, where established and budding names would be invited to run a stall during the two-day event to present their work and practice to the crowd. johnson banks had chosen to run a post office with stacks of alphabetical postcards to intrigue the visitors. Featuring letters from A to Z, the cards enable comers to actually 'send a letter' to your nearest and dearest. ■◤

Design: johnson banks, Hanna Sunden // Client: V&A Village fete

HUNTING LODGE

➤■ Hunting Lodge sells designer toys and clothing. To convey the playfulness and unique-ness of the shop, a set of simple yet colourful characters inspired by Flannelgraph, the once state-of-the-art storytelling medium popular among kindergartens, was created using felt. Like children's drawing with an innocent aesthetics in its most vibrant and delightful tone, the "animals" were photographed and developed into a pattern that could probably cheer up any kids and moms. ■■◀

⊙ *Design: Commando Group AS // Client: Hunting Lodge*

MY PORTFOLIO

▶▬ Not long after graduation and freelancing as a textile screen-printer, Mika Nash decided to turn her attention to surface design and illustration. While standard formats were not exactly practical to showcase her tactile work samples, Nash created a portfolio box that would be easy to update, inviting to look at and, above all, fun to explore. Selected textile products were made into 3D rabbit-teddy or neatly folded next to small booklets of illustrations to give a better idea of projects which she could get involved. ▬◀

◉ Design: Mika Nash

MEAT PACKING IN-HOUSE PROMO

▶■▬ Having recently moved into an old butcher's workshop, ilovedust began to lend its shop facing identity to its environment by manually screenprinting the butchers aprons and tea towels, wrapped alongside a perfect bound book to reveal the studio's latest work, in light-weight news print, secured together with twine. The promotional packs were sent to showcase and inform their new and existing clients of the unique makeover in East London. ■▬◀

◉ Design: ilovedust

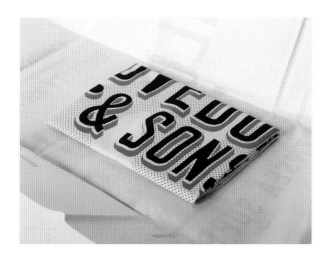

豊かなイメージが湧いてくるような、
新鮮なインスピレーションを与えるような、
インパクトのあるアクセサリーを
世界中からセレクトしています。
"ここにしかない"特別なジュエリー、
芸術的価値のあるアンティークやリバイバル。
もちろんデイリーなものから、
ハードなテイストのコスチューム系までが幅広く集結。
アクセサリーを遊ぶことから始まる、
そんな新しいスタイリングを可能にするお店です。

mahna mahna accent

Business hours 10:00-19:00
Regular holiday : National holiday / Sunday
E-mail : accent@mahna.co.jp
〒107-0062 東京都港区南青山 5-12-28 メゾン青山ビル 301
301 5-12-28 Minami-Aoyama, Minato-ku, Tokyo Japan 107-0062
Tel +81(0)3-3409-3118
Fax +81(0)3-3409-2982
http://www.mahna.co.jp/

mahna mahna gold

水晶に細工最高のブラシゴルド。
ランジェリーは本番のパリを中心に、
コスチュームは国内では手に入らない
"旬"をタイムリーにセレクトしている。
普に氷晶は本選としてスタイリングと
遊び人たちをくらいに楽しい個展・窓待を
体験できるライトアップです。

Business hours 10:00-19:00
Regular holiday : National holiday / Sunday
E-mail : gold@mahna.co.jp
〒107-0062 東京都港区南青山 5-12-28 メゾン青山ビル 401
401 5-12-28 Minami-Aoyama, Minato-ku, Tokyo Japan 107-0062
Tel +81(0)3-3409-2982
Fax +81(0)3-3409-2982
http://www.mahna.co.jp/

✤ MAHNA MAHNA

mahna mahna is paradise for professional stylists, a resourceful mart for fashion items for rent or sale for photo shoots. More like a collectible memo pad than traditional corporate items, the boutique's business cards featured a delicious combination of dress, shoes and jewellery to open dialogues at the card-exchanging scenes. The shop card resembled clothes tag so as to suggest mahna mahna as fashion boutique.

◉ Design: Three & Co. // Client: mahna mahna co.,ltd. // Photography: Norihisa Yamane // Styling: Kyoko Amano

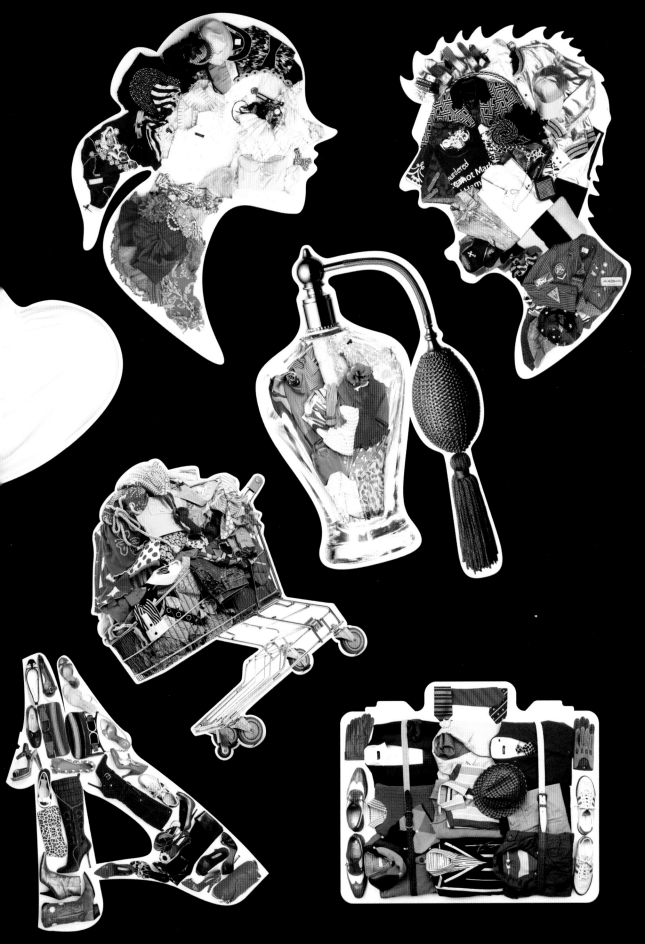

FILA PRINT CAMPAIGN

➤▬ Manga art is Japanese's second language. Its expressions and style have made up a major part of the Japanese culture, values and aesthetics for hundreds of age. For a strong connection between sports, fashion, young Japanese and FILA for the brand's spring-and-summer collection in 2010, Alex Trochut derived three energetic manga illustrations on three shoots, based on the common sounds and equipments symbolic of golf, tennis and fitness, to associate the corresponding apparel lines. Corporate colours of FILA were used to create resonance with the brand. ▬◄

⊙ Design: Alex Trochut // Client: FILA Japan // Photography: Mr. Kikuma // Special Credit: Katsunori "Katz" Sasaki (Agency AD)

SHUSH IMAGES IDENTITY SUITE

➤■ The name 'Shush Images' was created to work as a mental trigger for the library service that photographer Sandii McDonald would want to include as her new service offerings. With an intension to capture the attention of her client base in the creative sector, a strapline 'Louder than words' was developed around the simple yet powerful nature of pictures – if 'a picture talks louder than words'. The tension within the idea was extended to its soft types and fluorescent backgrounds to cohere the theme. ■■◄

◉ *Design: Everything Design // Client: Shush Images*

EVERYTHING XMAS TSHIRT

➤■ What would you get for a person who already has 'Everything' for Christmas? Blaming Christmas for creeping up on them while the new office was flat out working on client projects, Everything's first Christmas gift for friends was an extension of what they have already established on their website – building messages around their new name. The recipients would make sense of the message once they pulled out the shirt with the studio's name, "Everything". ■■◄

◉ *Design: Everything Design*

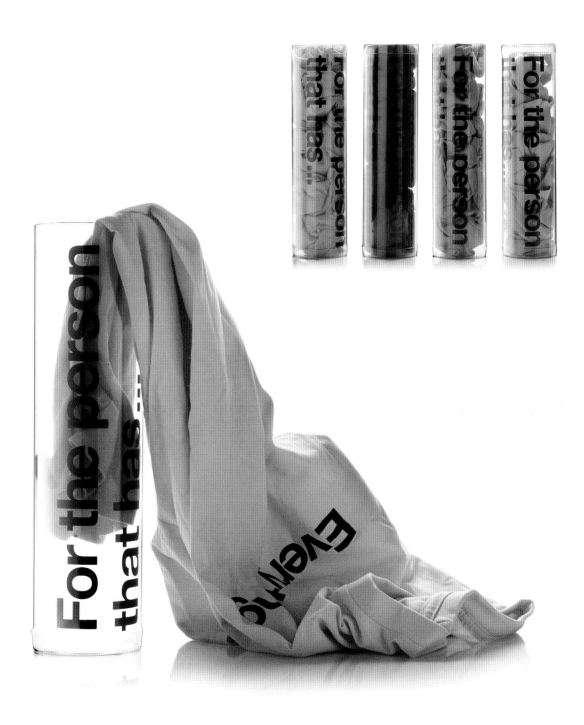

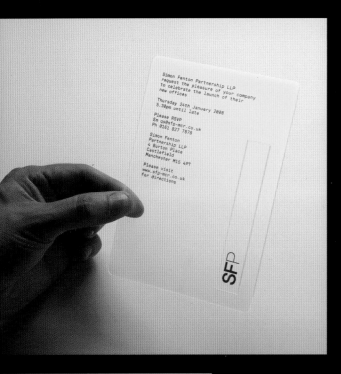

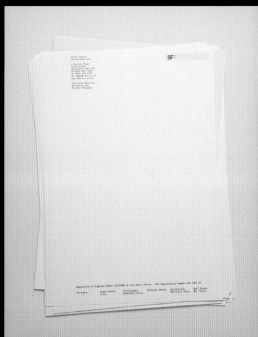

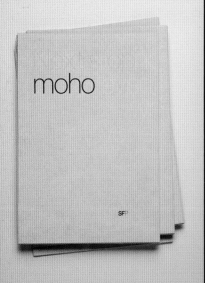

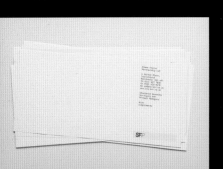

SFP REBRANDING & NEW OFFICE PARTY INVITE

▶■ Simon Fenton Partnership is a group of chartered surveyors and project managers based in Manchester established since 1988. As when their new office awaited the team to move in, the group also took the chance to renew their identity featuring their initials on a bright yellow stick along with a marketing suite. The new identity was incorporated into their new office launch party invitation made of Perspex, with a detachable logo stick. Honourable guests were asked to present the stick as they attend the event. ■◀

◉ *Design: B&W Studio // Client: Simon Fenton Partnership*

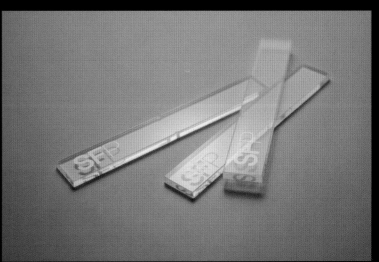

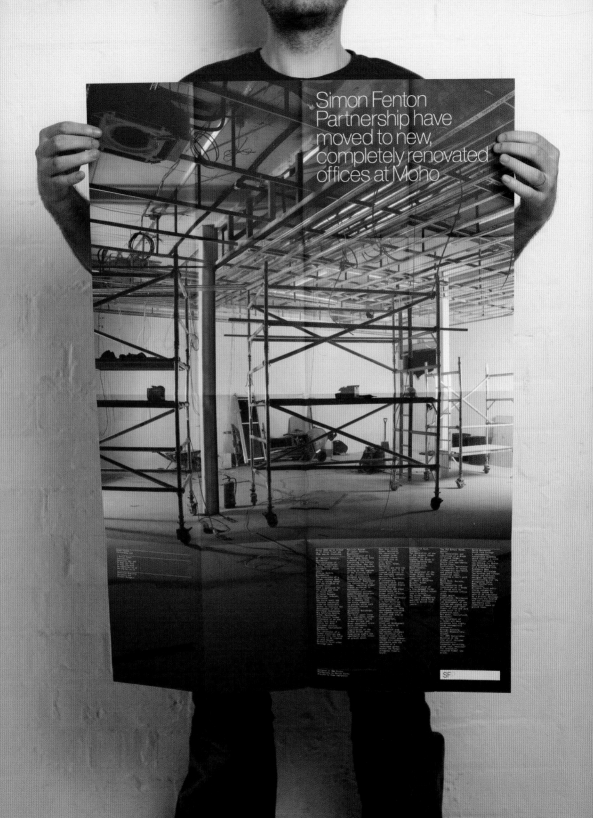

Simon Fenton
Partnership have
moved to new,
completely renovated
offices at Moho

☒ SEESAW CHRISTMAS
☒ CHOCOLATES

▶■ For a sweet sampling of what Seesaw Design is capable of, a packet of Christmas Chocolates cast from custom chocolate moulds was made, branded and wrapped in the practice's creative interpretation, stock before sent off to existing and potential clientele.Selecting and creating a new chocolate flavour (dark chocolate with cranberries and coconut) with The Chocolate Tailors, one of Seesaw's clients, was one of the high points. The chocolates has allowed Seesaw to display multidisciplinary aspects and engaged all staff and a new client with rewarding response and results. ■◀

⊙ *Design: Seesaw Design // Chocolate Supply: The Chocolate Tailors // Copywriting: See Strategic*

Oh it can't be that time of year again…can it?

You know we've been so busy it took, an overly brisk walk through the supermarket humming Jingle Bell Rock, past a stand of very cheap pens and really huge uncooked turkeys to realise, with a rush of shock, horror and awe, yet another festive season is upon us.

Another year older, another year wiser if anyone likes to know all the very best, Christmas is a time for reflection in the worst of more than a few.

A lantern would be the acme of more festive wisdom, a concept hope might come without a spare.

The new best. The Chocolate whatever lets...

Just as for those reasons we thought it might be worth, now let's not go home in 2011 New, adult, exciting chocolate is now more exciting and surprising.

• Brad & Sharp
• Mellin &
• Zig & XII
• Milk Chocolate

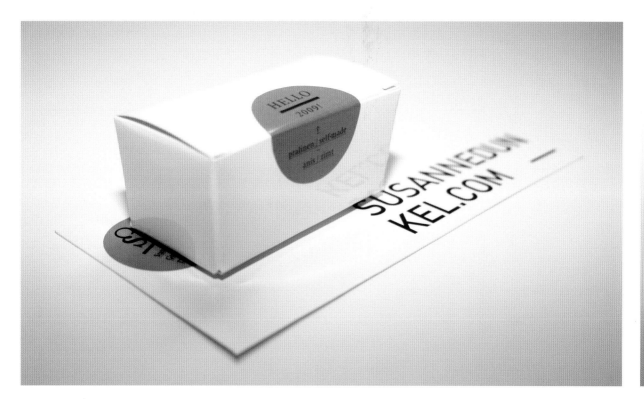

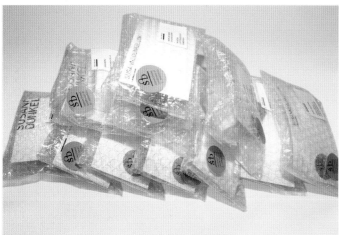

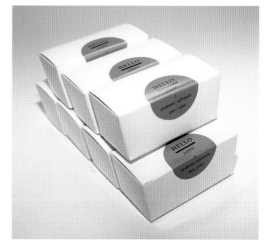

HELLO 2009

▶■ Susanne Dunkel was a German freelance designer based in Cologne who had just finished her diploma with a wish to thank all her friends and clients for their great inspiration and cooperation in between. 'Hello' came as a perfect media to express thanks and to formally publish her name as a professional designer in practice. The designer's initials and website were printed over the homemade white chocolate tiles friendly supported by café Törtchen Törtchen in Cologne and the packaging labels and flyer for dispatch. ■■◀

◉ *Design: Susanne Dunkel*

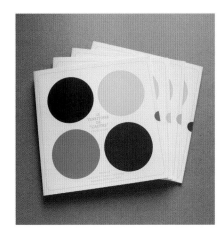

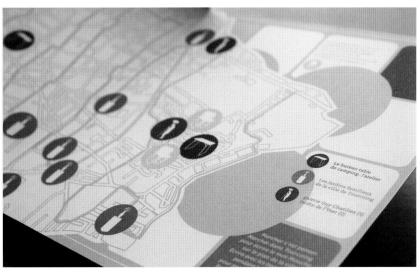

⚜ LE TERRITOIRE DE "L'AUTRE" – CÉLINE AHOND

➤■■ Like a roll-and-move game with loose cards and a map, the print project was made to introduce Céline Ahond and her work after her one-year residency at Galerie Guy Chatiliez. Ahond's projects were mostly colourful objects installation in public areas and performances involving local residence, so instead of a simple summary, sebastien lordez adopted an interactive format, using the same palettes, in continuity with her work. It was also an attractive tool to open conversations and invite audience's participation in the artist's work. ■■◄

◉ Design: sebastien lordez // Client: Galerie Guy Chatiliez // Photography: sebastien lordez, Gabrielle Degrugillier // Special Credits: Céline Ahond, Lucille Dautriche, François-Thibaut Pencenat, Quentin Sagot

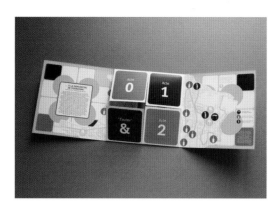

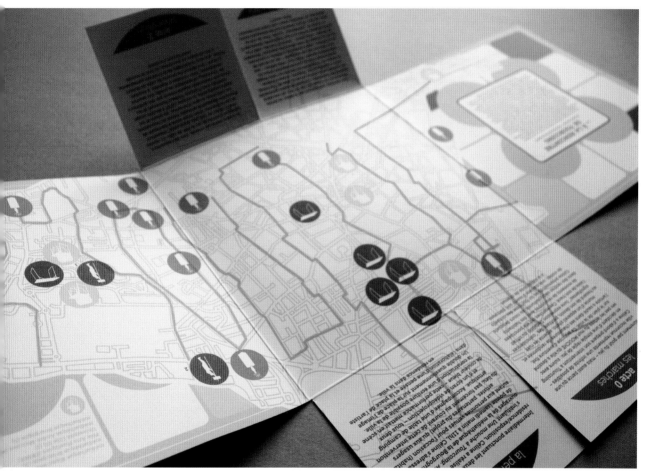

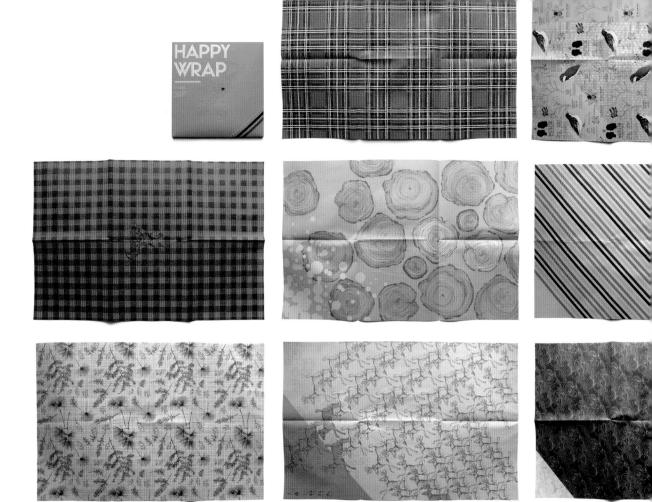

HAPPY WRAP

 Happy wrap has been Hemlock Printers' annual holiday gift for their clients for the past seven years. Each year a different firm will be invited to design the wrapper. Turnstyle was tasked for 2010's design. Definitely looking for ideas that would clearly be winter-themed and reflection of aesthetic prints, the team created eight designs with vivid references to the season to be printed into four doubled-sided wrappers. The whole set was tied together, with hints of the first wrapper revealed through the die-cut nose of the blind-embossed Rudolph on the front. ■■◄

◉ *Design: Turnstyle // Client: Hemlock Printers*

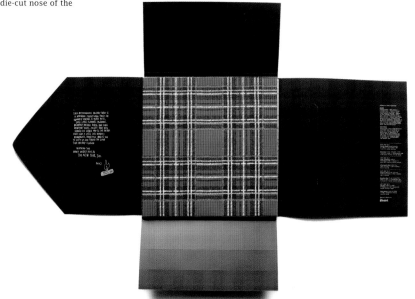

C p nh g n
Parts.

☙ COPENHAGEN PARTS

➤■■ Designed by Goodmorning Technology, the name and logo of "Copenhagen Parts" references the way people source different parts to construct their perfect bike. The iconic, quirky and crisp identity was devised as a rather stylish graphic presentation of the brand, established by a group of bike enthusiast-designers, and its innovative lifestyle biking gear offerings. Bike Porter was among their first product to introduce bicycle connoisseurs. ■■◀

⊙ *Design: Goodmorning Technology // Client: Copenhagen Parts*

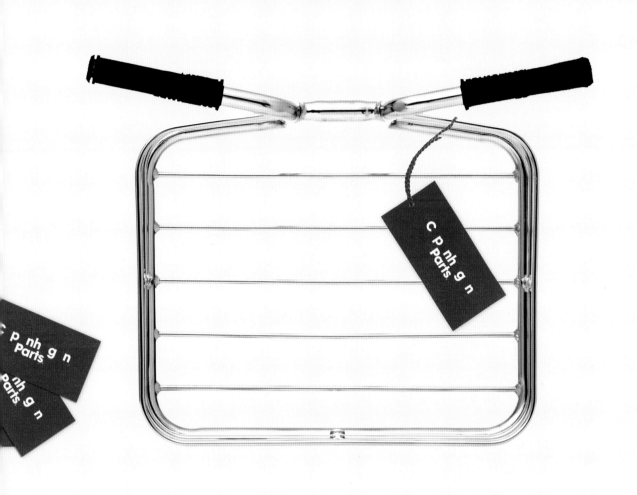

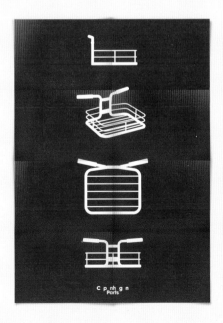

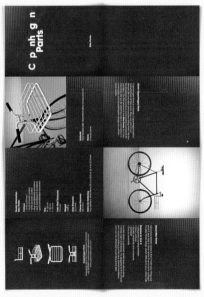

ASYLUM TOTE BAGS

▶▬ Affiliated with Asylum, a design practice in Singapore, Asylum Shop does not only retail arts and design but also double as a gallery and creative space for the workshop. Promoting the store as somewhere for inspirations and creative platform for exchanging ideas, Asylum specially designed a few prints for the shop's own shopping bag to coordinate the theme. The store offers a curation of products ranging from fashion, books, art and experimental music, with highlights on local artists and their own creative products. ▬◀

⊙ Design: Asylum // Client: Asylum Shop // Photography: Shooting Gallery

HELLO MONDAY — A GREAT DAY TO START THE WEEK

▶■■ Hello Monday was introducing alternative views to look at 'Monday', first day of a work week, telling stories about 'Monday' on the darker side and wonderful things on the brighter. Rather than displaying the creative agency's accomplishments on the double-sided poster, Hello Monday went for honest stories and let viewers decide which side of views more genuinely described the day to start the week. ■■◀

◉ *Design: Hello Monday*

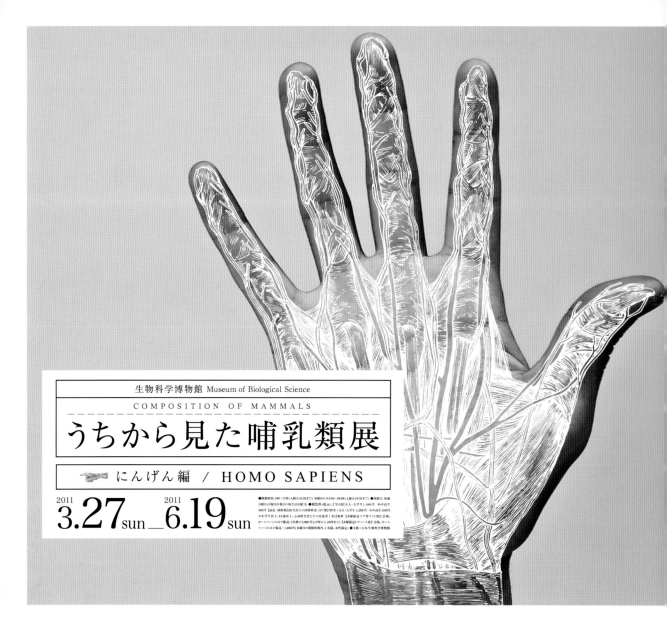

 # COMPOSITION OF MAMMALS

▶■ Composition of Mammal is an exhibition that studied the anatomy of mammals with displays of taxidermy and skulls. To promote its happening at the Museum of Biological Science, a series of posters were designed to evoke a pure fascination for the complexity and structures of mammals' bodily structure, such as the blood vessels and bones by printing diagram-like illustrations over photographed bodies. The project was a graduation project of Wataru Yoshida for Tama Art University. Both the event and venue were fictitious in this project. ■◀

◉ *Design: Wataru Yoshida*

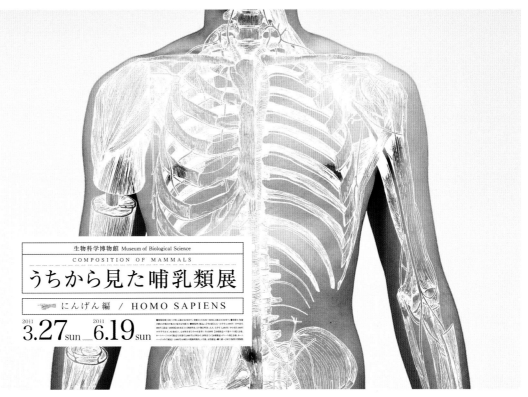

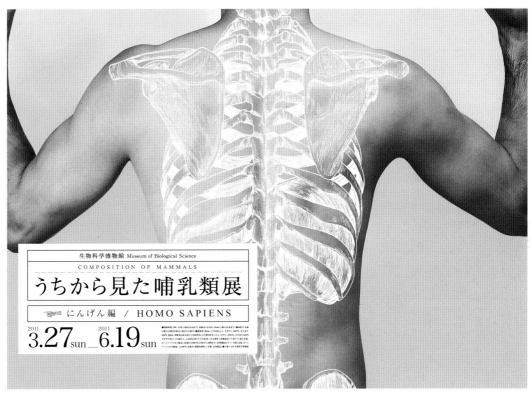

生物科学博物館 Museum of Biologie

COMPOSITION OF MAM

うちから見た哺

🐾 陸の哺乳類編 / MAMMA

2011
7.17sun ___ 2011
9.25sun

生物科学博物館 Museum of Biological Science

COMPOSITION OF MAMMALS

うちから見た哺乳類展

🐾 海の哺乳類編 / MAMMALS OF SEA

2011
10.16sun ___ 2011
12.18sun

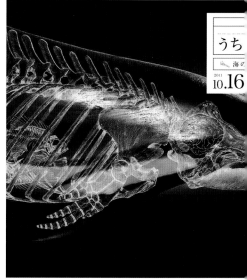

うち

🐾 海の

2011
10.16

SWAAN + CHRISTOS
USA TOUR

➤▬ Swaan and Christos were two alternative country and indie-pop songwriters setting to tour the States to play their respective repertories together on the piano and guitar. To highlight the composition of the duet and the interactions, animals native to North America were pictured and manipulated with digital effects to reference the music genres. Details of the musician and the tour event were saved for a clean appearance and replaced by a simple URL where images and songs were available for reference. ▬◄

◉ *Design: Mark Brooks Graphik Design // Client: Maarten Swaan*

SWAAN +
CHRISTOS
2011 USA
TOUR

VISIT US AT
WWW.MYSPACE.COM/SWAANCHRISTOS
FOR TOUR SCHEDULLE

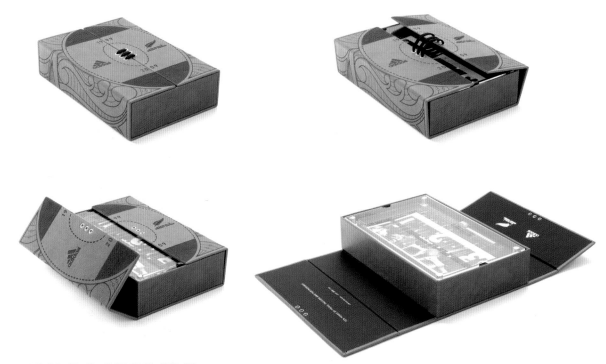

10 YEARS OF PRIDE, PASSION & PARTNERSHIP

A gift set was specially tailored to celebrate the ten years of successful partnership between adidas and the New Zealand Rugby Union, All Blacks. Also designed as a tribute to this passionate sport, key elements including a personalised mouthguard, rugby shoe studs, rubber band, photos that witnessed time, a fabric-bound book and a game plan etched on plexi glass were delivered in a leather box fastened with a rugby shoe lace. The box, numbered, was impressed with a indigenous New Zealand "Moko" marking, drawn by a player of All Blacks.

Design: Paperlux GmbH // Client: The Art Box Collection Berlin, adidas International // Photography: Michael Pfeiffer

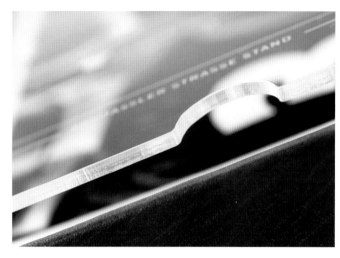

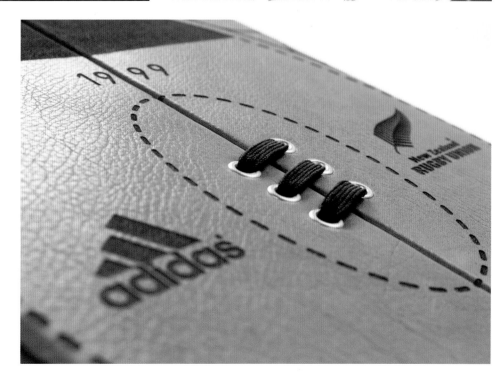

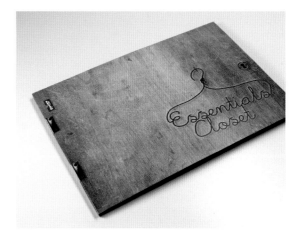

⚜ LEVI'S CLOSET

▶▬ Every wardrobe should at least contain a few "must-have" pieces, so the "Levi's Essentials" was introduced to inspire fashion editors with some recommended choices available in store. A miniature wardrobe with a loose set of jeans and tops made of cardboard and embossed paper was attached in the press mailer as an everyday little game to stand on the editors' desks. ▬◀

 Design: Melville Brand Design // Client: Häberlein & Mauerer (PR Agency), Levi Strauss & Co.

LEVI'S
COLOURED DENIM

▶■■ "Check my Colour! Heat me with your hand" was a simple call-for-action from Levi's to inform the press of their latest vibrant jeans collection during some winter months. The idea was to intrigue the recipients by covering the true spectrum of the new Coloured Denim with thermo-dynamic spot-colours, so colours would only come visible when heated by body warmth. Melville had undergone a rather bumpy road to get to this perfect result amid the longest and coldest ever winter in town. ■■◀

◉ *Design: Melville Brand Design // Client: Häberlein & Mauerer (PR Agency), Levi Strauss & Co.*

 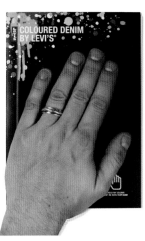  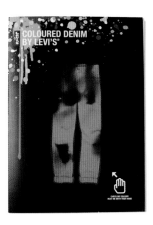

A

Airmail

Bringing lightness
to everyday objects

29 May / 28 June 2009

GOODD

11 james morrison street
Glasgow G1 5PE
0141-552-6777
info@good-d.com

OSCAR DIAZ/ INCA STARZINSKY/
JOCHEM FAUDET/ BERNADETTE
DEDDENS/ SIMON DONALD/ TIM
PARSONS/ JUDITH VAN DEN BOOM/
DAVID WEATHERHEAD/ HENNY
VAN NISTELROOY/ LUKA STEPAN/
BAS KOOLS/ STEPHEN REED

FROM: **A** Airmail — OSCAR DIAZ / INCA STARZINSKY/ JOCHEM FAUDET/ BERNADETTE DEDDENS/ JUDITH VAN DEN BOOM/ DAVID WEATHERHEAD/ HENNY VAN NISTELROOY/ LUKA STEPAN/ BAS KOOLS/ STEPHEN REED

TO: **GOODD**
11 JAMES MORRISON
STREET
GLASGOW   G1 5PE

0141 - 552 6777
info@good-d.com

ITEM :   PRICE :

FROM: **A** Airmail — OSCAR DIAZ / INCA STARZINSKY/ JOCHEM FAUDET/ BERNADETTE DEDDENS/ JUDITH VAN DEN BOOM/ DAVID WEATHERHEAD/ HENNY VAN NISTELROOY/ LUKA STEPAN/ BAS KOOLS/ STEPHEN REED

TO: **GOODD**
11 JAMES MORRISON
STREET
GLASGOW   G1 5PE

0141 - 552 6777
info@good-d.com

ITEM : *gravity*   PRICE : 89.-

AIRMAIL EXHIBITION GRAPHICS

▬▬ Airmail was a collective exhibition where 13
designers, including Oscar Diaz, would display and
sell their products at Glasgow-based design shop
and gallery GOODD. Where budget was small, a
multi-purpose poster that doubled as a catalogue and
invitation was printed. Keeping it visually simple and
straightforward, the graphics made reference to the
Royal Mail printed labels, with reds and blues commonly found on airmail envelopes. A price tag label
was also designed to be shared among the participating designers in black and white. ▬◄

⊙ *Design: Oscar Diaz Studio, Henny van Nistelroy // Client:
GOODD Gallery, Glasgow*

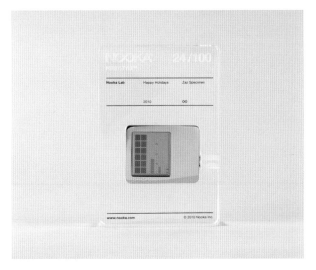

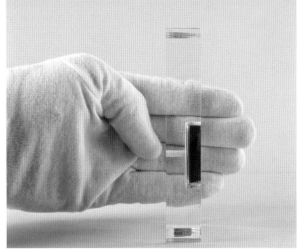

NOOKA
HOLIDAY GIFT

➤■ US fashion brand Nooka defined itself as a story of "one brand's quest for universal language" via visuals and forms. Zaz watch, featuring a transparent screen with the brand's signature digital time display, was one of the brand's pursuit. For a unique and memorable greeting during the holiday season, Nooka "froze" its timepiece into a block of "ice" as a gift for the brand's friends and family. Each acrylic block was etched with a short description of the specimen and the edition number (out of 100) next to Nooka's logo design. ■◀

⊙ *Design: Nooka Inc.*

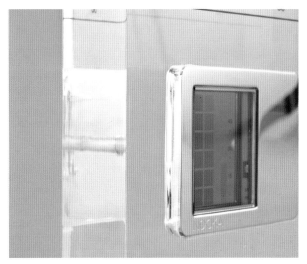

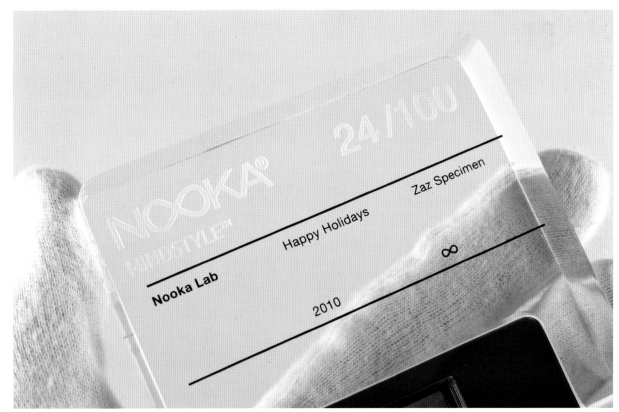

the kitchen films®

THE KITCHEN

➤■■ The Kitchen Films is a low-cost advertising production company with a clientele who are mainly in the advertising, television and audiovisual sector. For their identity update, Ruiz created a game among all identity pieces, where individual items, e.g. CDs and business cards, can interact with accompanied items, such as the keep cases and envelopes. Using a minimalist visual code, the overall identity forms a fully-equiped kitchen model. ■■◄

⊙ *Design: ruiz+company // Client: The Kitchen Films*

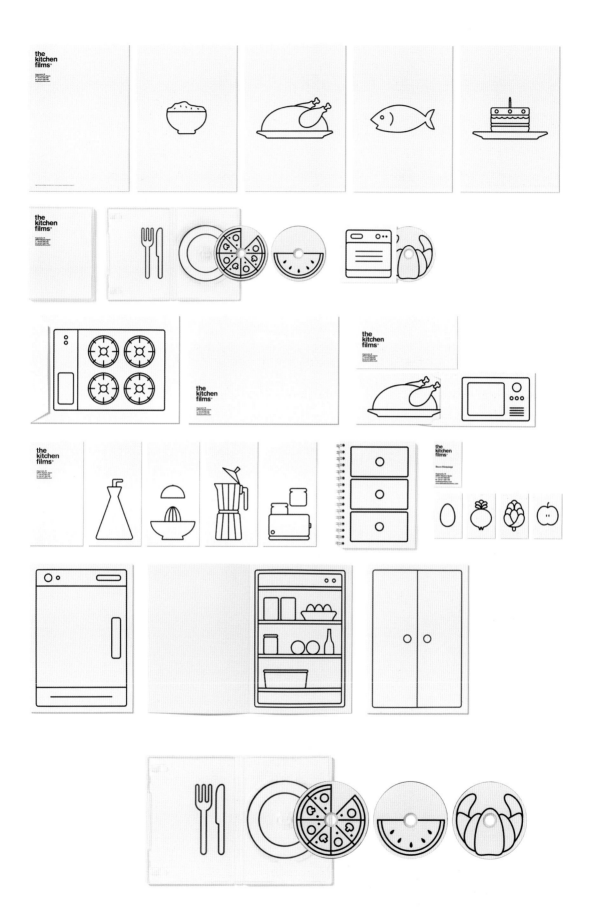

4

APRIL

Name: Ziggy
Age: 1½ years old
Tail Measurement: 10"
Eye Color: Blue
Pet Peeve: Other animals, he thinks he's human.

Ziggy loves toys! He was returned to the pet store and I got him by fate.

Floral Print Mini Dress with Saring Sleeve Detail (UMX100)

4

1 / 2
3 / 4 / 5 / 6 / 7 / 8 / 9
10 / 11 / 12 / 13 / 14 / 15 / 16
17 / 18 / 19 / 20 / 21 / 22 / 23
24 / 25 / 26 / 27 / 28 / 29 / 30

FEBRUARY

Name: Oscar
Age: 6–8 years old
Tail Measurement: 12"
Eye Color: Green
Pet Peeve: Oscar does not like it when people blow air in his face, it messes up his pretty whiskers!

I didn't know he was blind until after I adopted him! He has cheated death twice! OMG!

Regatta Blazer with Striped Trim (UMV100)
White Shirt Dress

2

2

1 / 2 / 3 / 4 / 5
6 / 7 / 8 / 9 / 10 / 11 / 12
13 / 14 / 15 / 16 / 17 / 18 / 19
20 / 21 / 22 / 23 / 24 / 25 / 26
27 / 28

12

2 / 3
4 / 5 6 / 7 8 / 9 / 10
11 / 12 / 13 / 14 / 15 / 16 / 17
18 / 19 / 20 / 21 / 22 / 23 / 24
25 / 26 / 27 / 28 / 29 / 30 / 31

DECEMBER

12

Name: Patoofie
Age: 2 ½ years old
Tail Measurement: 10"
Eye Color: Yellow
Pet Peeve: Being carried. Too undignified.

Rescued from the Staten Island Pageant Contest in New York.

Reproduction #: 69.Fishtail Parka (Arrdore)

UNITED BAMBOO CAT CALENDAR 2011

➤▬▬ United Bamboo is a fun and innovative fashion maker who welcomes bold attempts. So a portion of UB's ready-to-wear wardrobe was duplicated in miniature, worn on top of some restive cats' own furry coat for a very unusual fashion shoot. The limited edition calendar features 12 pages of French fold high gloss sheets, with calendar months blind embossed onto each full bleed cat image. A butcher paper sleeve was made to go with the print, with silk-screened numbers and patterns on the back. ▬◀

◉ *Design: Studio Lin // Client: United Bamboo // Photography: Noah Sheldon*

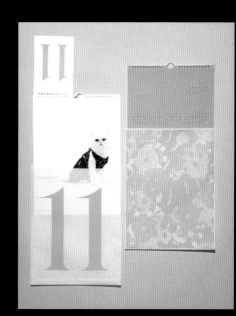

3

1 / 2 / 3 / 4 / 5
6 / 7 / 8 / 9 / 10 / 11 / 12
13 / 14 / 15 / 16 / 17 / 18 / 19
20 / 21 / 22 / 23 / 24 / 25 / 26
27 / 28 / 29 / 30 / 31

6

1 / 2 / 3 / 4
5 / 6 / 7 / 8 / 9 / 10 / 11
12 / 13 / 14 / 15 / 16 / 17 / 18
19 / 20 / 21 / 22 / 23 / 24 / 25
26 / 27 / 28 / 29 / 30

3

MARCH

Name: Egon
Age: 7 years old
Tail Measurement: 12"
Eye Color: Amber
Pet Peeve: Egon doesn't like to be left out of dinner parties. Whenever guests come over for a meal, he will meow mournfully until we pull up an extra chair for him.

Egon lived with us abroad in Istanbul for a few months. We had a Turkish neighbor, Ahmet, who looked after him for a weekend while we were traveling. Upon returning, Ahmet had many nice things to say about his time with Egon, all in broken English. It sounded like they had a great time. Ahmet concluded his story by saying "I love your cat. He is very, um, I don't know the word — ssss!!" I suggested, "Fluffy? Playful?" "No, no. None of these." Ahmet said. "Oh, I remember the word. Ugly. Your cat is very ugly." It's true. Egon is very ugly-cute.

Floral Summer Dress (1997/8)

6

JUNE

Name: Bruce
Age: 11 months
Tail Measurement: 11"
Eye Color: Yellow/Green
Pet Peeve: Bruce doesn't like being picked up and held. He especially hates being held like a baby, with his belly facing up.

Bruce and his brothers and sisters were little kitten babies living in the empty lot next to my apartment building. I started to feed them, because it was cold outside and they looked very skinny. After a week, I started petting them and tried to pick them up. Bruce didn't run away when I petted him and let me push him up for a few seconds, so I took him home.

Sleeveless Jacquardo Shirt (S/S/S)
Suede Shorts

7

7

1 / 2
3 / 4 / 5 / 6 / 7 / 8 / 9
10 / 11 / 12 / 13 / 14 / 15 / 16
17 / 18 / 19 / 20 / 21 / 22 / 23
24 / 25 / 26 / 27 / 28 / 29 / 30
31

7

JULY

Name: TJ a.k.a. Thomas Jefferson
Age: 12 years old
Tail Measurement: 11"
Eye Color: Yellow/Green/Black
Pet Peeve: TJ doesn't like if there are no options.
She often freaks out if she feels stuck in a room,
so we need to make sure doors are always open
for her.

*TJ's mom was a Brooklyn alley cat. My friend was
watching her one day she delivered many kitten,
so I adopted the most fabulous looking kitty, TJ!
She is an original United Bamboo mascot cat and
later, mascot Nori!*

"Jungle" Print Evening Dress with Bowtie Detail (UKD081)

1

JANUARY

Name: Radley
Age: 5 years old
Tail Measurement: 10"
Eye Color: Brown
Pet Peeve: Radley's pet peeve is the litter box.
He thinks he just may chase him—he doesn't
understand its his own alive. So he runs out fast after
doing his biznes and does circles around the
apt to make sure no Mr. Hanky is following.

*Radley was cat-sited by Karen O of the Yeah
Yeah Yeahs.*

Sequined Razor-Back Cocktail Dress (UKD108)

1

1
2 / 3 / 4 / 5 / / 8
9 / 10 / 11 / 12 / 13 / 14 / 15
16 / 17 / 18 / 19 / 20 / 21 / 22
23 / 24 / 25 / 26 / 27 / 28 / 29
30 / 31

 # RIBBONESIA

▶▬ Ribbonesia is an art project where artist and illustrator, Baku Maeda, explores and extends the form and applications of ribbon knots to animal sculptures other than traditional gift packaging. With emphases on the unique expressions of mixed rayon bands, a minimal approach was taken to stress the artwork themselves. The 16-item collection was photographed and produced into individual identity and corporate products, including greeting mailers and coasters, marked with Ribbonesia's logo made of elegant ribbon twists. ▬◀

◉ *Design: COMMUNE // Client: Baku Maeda*

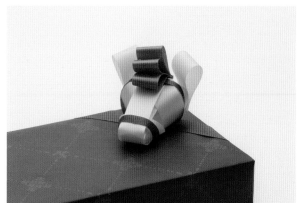

⚜ ❋ INVITATIONS & TEASER CAMPAIGN FOR JUST B.

➤▬ Just B. is a Dutch fashion brand that has distinguished itself with its designs for independent, cosmopolitan women. Responsible for Just B.'s integral brand concept, Smel's goal for the brand's seasonal invitations and teaser campaign was to authentically convey a personal and nostalgic feel and turn a smile upon the recipients face. Stylishly and perfectly executed, each invitation was a clean and powerful product, combining simple visuals and a relatively complex folding or printing technique. ▬◄

◉ *Design: Smel // Client: Just B.*

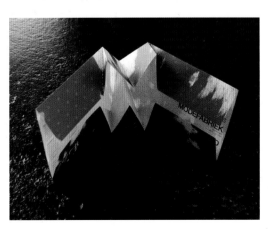

 # CORE

➤■ Core prides themselves on conversations rooted in the combination of art and design. While publishing the architecture students' yearly findings in topics surrounding architecture, design and social issues, the periodic also invites readers to get involved in the conversation as they read. Continuing on the tradition, the 2009 issue asked its readers to interpret topic sentence on the magazine cover, "No One Will __ This", to bring out their own views on the topics covered inside. ■■◀

⦿ *Design: Rob Schellenberg, Derek Hunt // Client: Iowa State University Architecture Program*

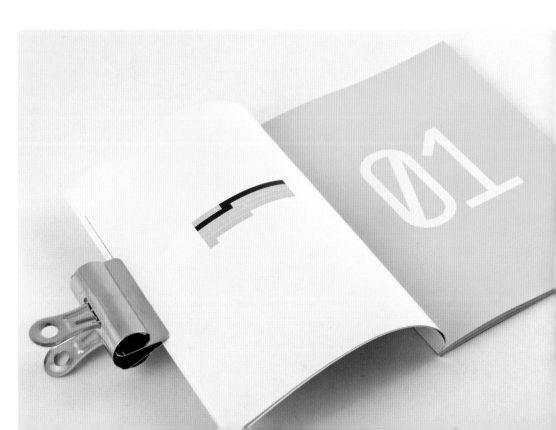

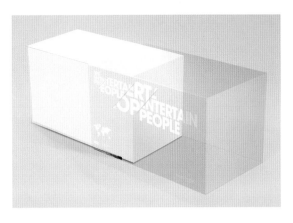

FOX INTERNATIONAL CHANNELS IDENTITY

➤■ A subsidiary of the Fox Entertainment Group, the Fox International Channels take a variety of brands to deliver entertainment to homes across Europe, Africa, Asia and Latin America. From the group's slogan "We Entertain People", DHNN (design has no name) derived a frame-by-frame concept, by breaking and combining moments of action and response into a dynamic movement, as the key visuals of the company's brand image. The electric images were produced into posters and corporate graphics, accompanied by seven spot colours to allude the channel brands it operates. ■◀

◉ *Design: DHNN (design has no name) // Client: Fox International Channels*

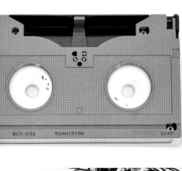

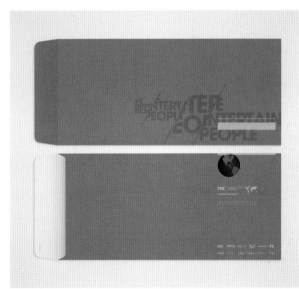

WE
ENTERTAIN
PEOPLE

 # THE FUTURE PERFECT POSTER

▶■ The Future Perfect Manhattan store was about to host an event to unveil an array of new home-styling products by selected local designers. The store wanted a giveaway with information about the event and designers, as well as its new location in town. The solution was more than just a poster pad featuring a neon yellow glue edge and a illustration of the physical storefront. The final product was intended to challenge viewers to give the poster a few folds and create an illusion of a dimensional miniature store of their own. ■■◀

⊙ *Design: Studio Lin // Client: The Future Perfect // Illustration: Dana Davis*

 LUFF

▶️■ Born with the formation of LUFF Association For The Promotion of Independent Cinema, the Lausanne Underground Film & Music Festival (LUFF) has been demonstrating the panoply of music creation and cinematography left in the shadow of the mainstream culture. Seeing a complete change in its management for its ninth edition, Demian Conrad introduced the nature of politics with a two-faced print, combining the human and monster faces to introduce the new management team. Everyone showed a side of human and monster as participants viewed the images with a filter glass. ■■◤

⊙ Design: DEMIAN CONRAD DESIGN // Client: Lausanne Underground Film & Music Festival //
Photography: Olivier Lovey // Copywriting: Maxime Pégatoquet

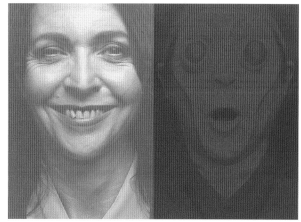

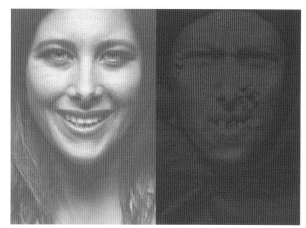
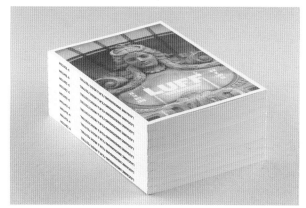

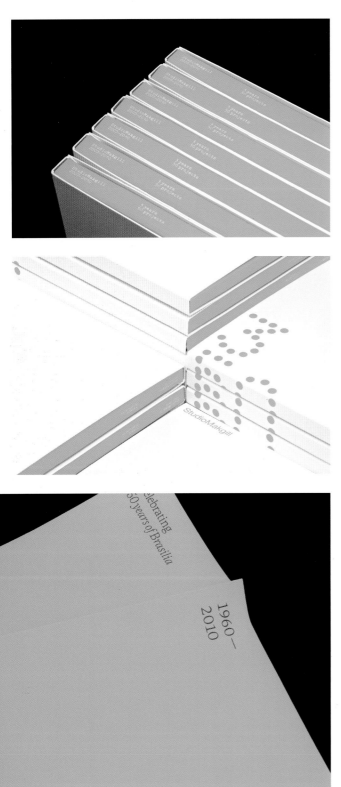

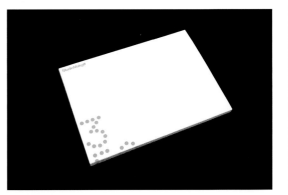

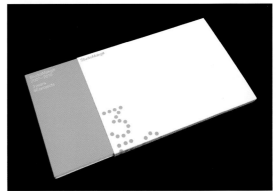

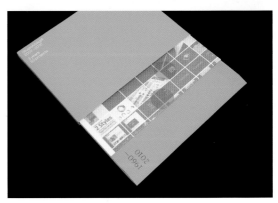

 3 YEARS
50 PROJECTS

▶■ Three years in business is no easy trajectory. Happening to have the studio's 50th project completed upon StudioMakgill's third birthday, a celebratory poster was produced to coincide with the introduction of "Brasilia Dice 50", created to mark Brasilia's 50 years of existence. StudioMakgill's portfolio were rolled out as greyscale thumbnails to ascent the numbers in dots of glowing green as a hint of connection. ■■◀

◉ *Design: StudioMakgill*

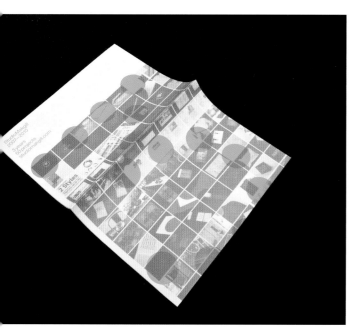

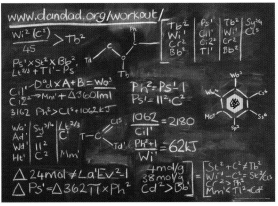

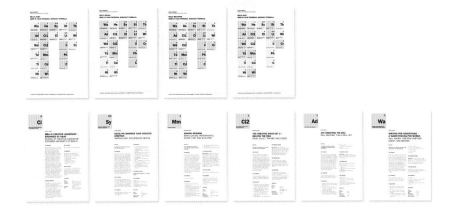

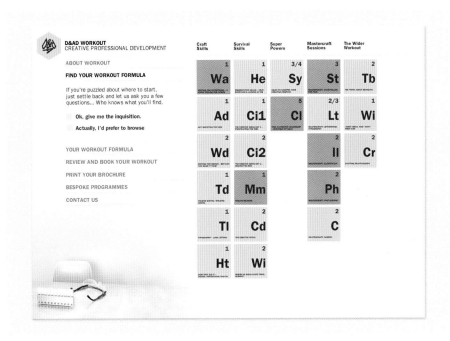

NAL DEVELOPMENT

D&AD WORKOUT

Established to promote excellence in Design and Advertising, D&AD Workout is a programme of workshops set to challenge the idea of professional development and metaphorically place attendees in a world of chemistry, where they can experiment with ideas and build knowledge. Applying the concept into its programmer, the new system sought users' attention by a collection of supporting advertising, direct mail and poster campaign. Course selection was made easy by organising into a periodic table divided by levels and skills.

⊙ *Design: A+B Studio // Client: D&AD*

CORE77 AWARDS ANNOUNCEMENT

➤■ Core77 is an online magazine dedicated to the practice and production of industrial design. After 16 years of bringing industrial updates to the global design community, the magazine had decided to launch its first ever annual design awards, kicked off with a poster-cum-invitation to announce the event. On the back of the invitation poster featured the a complete style guide for the new Core77 Design Awards identity and logo, allowing recipients to apprehend the process behind the creation of an identity. ■■◄

◉ *Design: Studio Lin // Client: Core77*

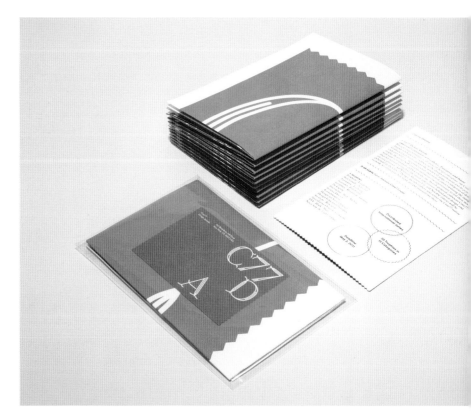

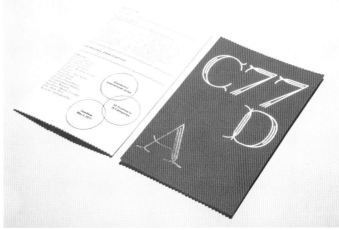

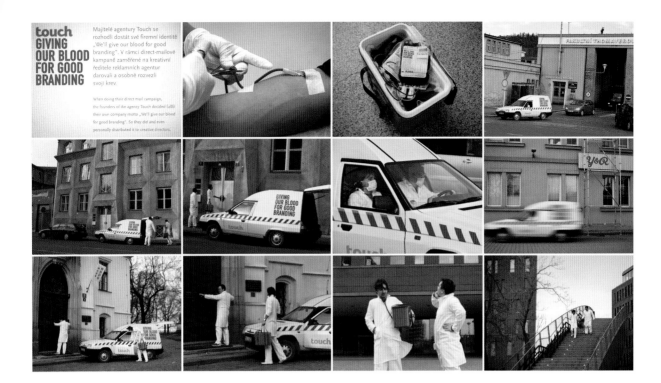

GIVE BLOOD
FOR GOOD BRANDING

➤▬ Blood donation saves life but giving blood can also attract publicity, according to Touch Branding. Handing out fake-blood bags as their mailers and the key visual of their corporate identity, the company created a simple brand message and excitement on multiple touchpoints. The blood bags were delivered to the creative directors of several advertising agencies in Prague by the hands of Touch Branding's owners in medical gowns and a branded delivery pickup. ▬◀

◉ *Design: Touch Branding*

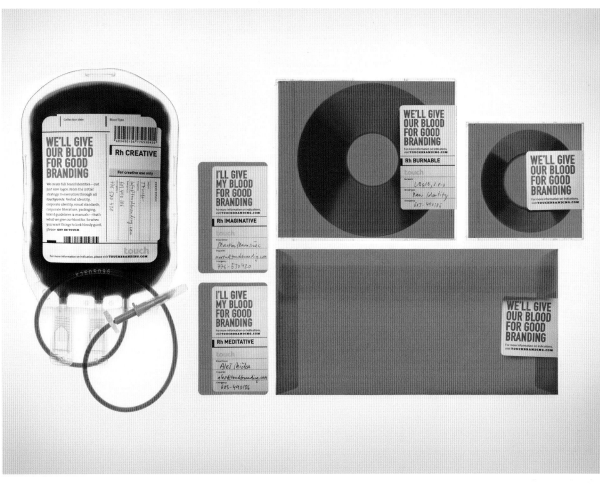

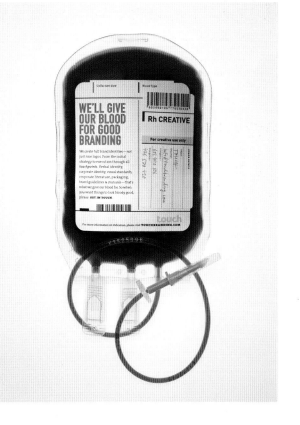

141

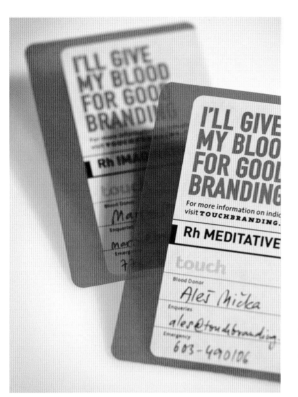

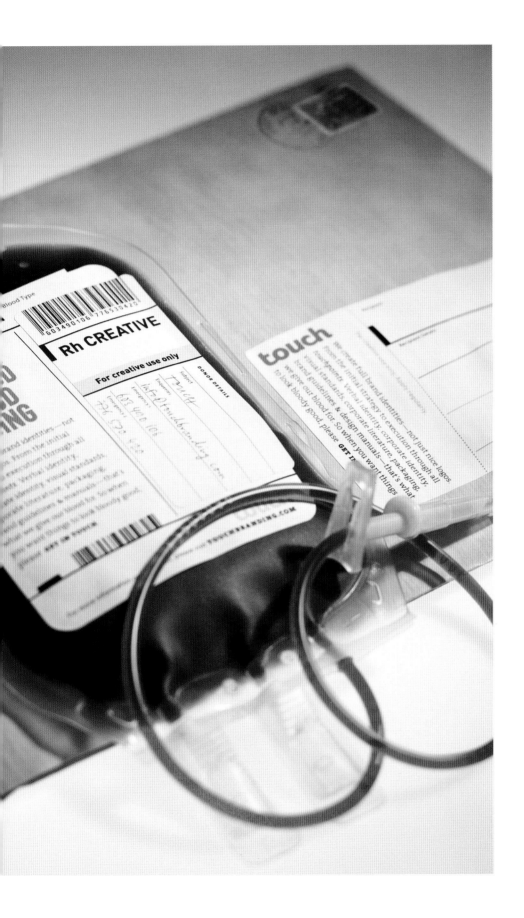

Rh CREATIVE

For creative use only

DONOR DETAILS

touch

We create full brand identities—not just nice logos
from the initial strategy to execution through all
its segments. Verbal identity, corporate identity,
visual guidelines, corporate literature, packaging,
brand guidelines & design manuals—that's what
we give our blood for. So when you want things
to look bloody good, please **GET IT**

603490106 775530420

WWW.TOUCHBRANDING.COM

143

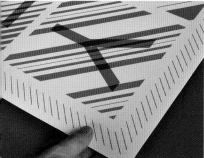

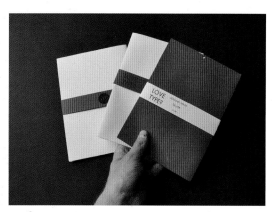

YTD
PROMOTIONAL
CAMPAIGN

Young Typographic Designers is where young creatives and fresh graduates could make connections with and gain exposure to people in the creative industry through community events and exhibitions. To highlight the organisation's focus on types and a sense of belonging, a series of corporate items and promotions were produced using types accompanied by minimal but bright graphic cues. The project was Angus MacPherson's university work in his final academic year.

◉ Design: Angus MacPherson

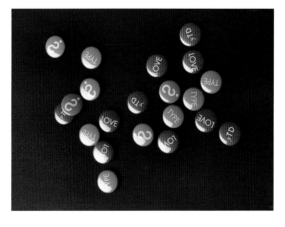

TURNSTYLE TOTES

▶■ Turnstyle stresses personality in design. But besides reflecting the design house's very own persona, prominence was also given to their approach in creative presentation in the tote bag designs made as the studio's holiday gift for their clients. "This is neither plastic, nor English", shouted out in German, French and Chinese, was a tongue-in-cheek nod to their environment-conscious solution. Only technorganic materials were used in the making of the bag. ■◀

◉ *Design: Turnstyle*

TURNSTYLE
PORTFOLIO
MAILER

▶■ Required to reflect Turnstyle's originality and enable updates, Turnstyle Portfolio
Mailer was a portfolio teaser with an express-
mail-packaging-styled pocket to house the studio's commissions and design samples printed
on a stack of postcards. Minimal and rigid,
the clipboard screenprinted and foil-stamped
with basic contact information and a hidden
"hello" on the front offers a cut-out handle, a
bonus feature that allowed recipients to carry
it around with pride. ■■◀

◉ *Design: Turnstyle*

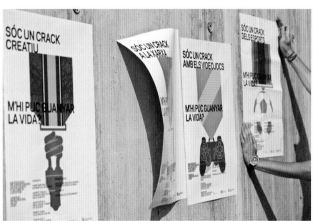

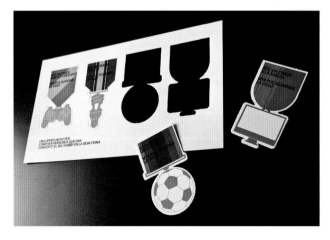

 SÓC UN CRACK

An educational campaign aiming to promote an entrepreneur spirit among young adults aged between 14 ad 30 was organised in Manlleu by the city's Economic Development Office. It was a programme of four events based on different professional fields related to technologies, sports, videogames production and creative-oriented jobs. Street posters and medal-styled sticker-flyers were produced using social network language to beam a fresh message among the young population. ■◤

◉ Design: Zoo Studio S.L. // Client: OPE Manlleu

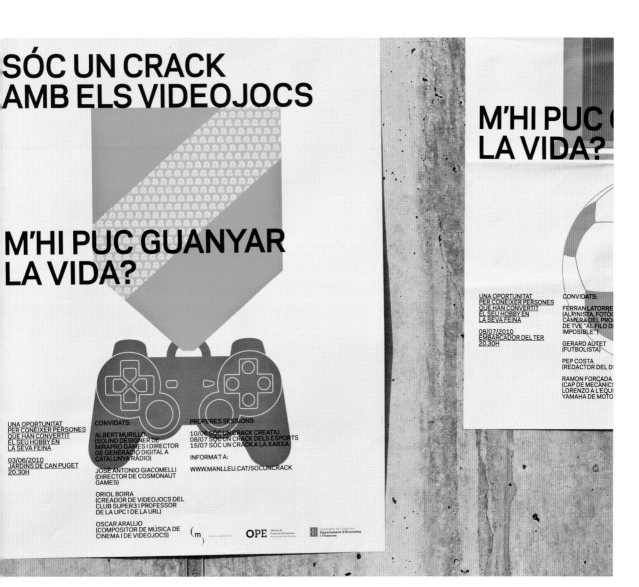

SÓC UN CRACK
AMB ELS VIDEOJOCS

M'HI PUC GUANYAR
LA VIDA?

UNA OPORTUNITAT
PER CONÈIXER PERSONES
QUE HAN CONVERTIT
EL SEU HOBBY EN
LA SEVA FEINA

03/06/2010
JARDINS DE CAN PUGET
20.30H

CONVIDATS:

ALBERT MURILLO
(SOUND DESIGNER DE
MIRAPRO GAMES I DIRECTOR
DE GENERACIÓ DIGITAL A
CATALUNYA RÀDIO)

JOSÉ ANTONIO GIACOMELLI
(DIRECTOR DE COSMONAUT
GAMES)

ORIOL BOIRA
(CREADOR DE VIDEOJOCS DEL
CLUB SUPER 3 I PROFESSOR
DE LA UPC I DE LA URL)

OSCAR ARAUJO
(COMPOSITOR DE MÚSICA DE
CINEMA I DE VIDEOJOCS)

PROPERES SESSIONS:

10/06 SÓC UN CRACK CREATIU
08/07 SÓC UN CRACK DELS ESPORTS
15/07 SÓC UN CRACK A LA XARXA

INFORMA'T A:

WWW.MANLLEU.CAT/SOCUNCRACK

M'HI PUC G
LA VIDA?

UNA OPORTUNITAT
PER CONÈIXER PERSONES
QUE HAN CONVERTIT
EL SEU HOBBY EN
LA SEVA FEINA

08/07/2010
EMBARCADOR DEL TER
20.30H

CONVIDATS:

FERRAN LATORRE
(ALPINISTA, FOTÒG
CÀMERA DEL PROG
DE TVE "AL FILO DE
IMPOSIBLE")

GERARD AUTET
(FUTBOLISTA)

PEP COSTA
(REDACTOR DEL DI

RAMON FORÇADA
(CAP DE MECÀNICS
LORENZO A L'EQUI
YAMAHA DE MOTO

151

NAO S/S CATALOGUES

nao's belief in "things of good quality are good at any time" are obvious in their handmade fashion products that use vintage fabrics on the theme of "links", as "the worth of good things link each other". The brand's spring-and-summer inspirations were narrated in two sets of catalogue cards. When put together, the cards were designed to set off recipients' imagination for a panorama of pollution-free nature with sunshine filtering through foliage. ◼◼◀

◉ *Design: mute // Client: nao // Styling: Satoshi Kanda*

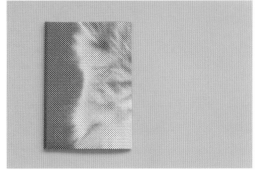

⊕ BELMACZ
❖ CATALOGUE 2010

⟩■■ Mind Design enjoyed making something a little more entertaining than just a pure product catalogue, so a cat named Rufus was introduced to 'model' in this jewellery catalogue. Rufus had reminded the team so much of the iconic villain in the James Bond movies that they decided to print the catalogue as a fold-out 'Most Wanted' poster. The catalogue itself was printed with an additional gold spot colour on the cover and all text. ■■◤

⊙ *Design: Mind Design // Client: Belmacz // Photography: Franck Allais*

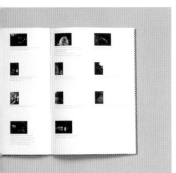

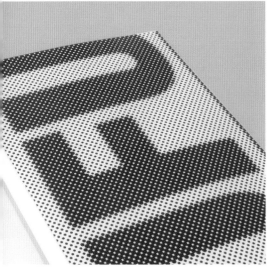

 LIMITED EDITION

◼◼ Made of Japan is an international style magazine that was introduced to celebrate the 60th anniversary of the Japanese sneaker brand Onitsuka Tiger. Smel was commissioned by Mulholland International. In collaboration with Sandor Lubbe and José Klap of Zoo Magazine and Mulholland International, a numbered limited edition including a gift box with the magazine, a pair of sneakers (Mexico 66 – 60 Years edition) and a jubilee T-shirt was developed. ◼◼◀

◉ *Design: Smel, Sandor Lubbe, José Klap // Client: Mulholland International // Publishing: ASICS Corporation*

ILOVEDUST BLACK BOOK

Held in a slipcase with unique die-cuts and a combination of gold and black foil stamps, the deceptively understated black book was ilovedust's latest promotional piece, loaded with an updated summary of illustration and design the studio had accomplished for global brands and local shops from their community. Despite the splendid content, innovative printing and finishing were added to create an even more eye-catching, personal and bespoke piece.

Design: ilovedust

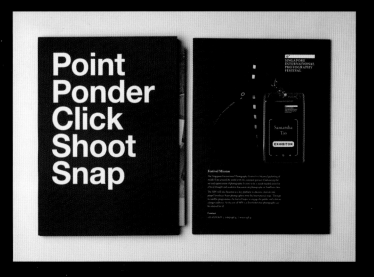

SIPF 2011

▶■■ The Singapore International Photography Festival (SIPF) is a worldwide biennial gathering of minds commonly pursuing the advancement and appreciation of photography. For the 2nd SIPF, the campaign identity stemmed from the idea of "putting together a show". A stack of prints, much like what a curator would be dealing with whilst selecting artworks, were used as the key visuals in the posters to tease out what to be expected during the show. Photography- and camera-themed prints were introduced on cotton shirts for sale at the event. ■■◀

◉ *Design: Asylum // Client: Singapore International Photography Festival // Photography: Lumina Photography*

SINGAPORE
INTERNATIONAL
PHOTOGRAPHY
FESTIVAL 2010

Human : Nature

15 Oct – 13 Nov 2010

The world is not coming to an end but nature is and perhaps with it humans.
The 2nd Singapore International Photography Festival explores this complex
relationship of dependence and destruction with exhibitions, workshops,
seminars and film screenings.

www.sipf.sg

Singapore International
Photography Festival 2010

Human : Nature

Abednego Trianto Kurniawan, Agnes Marszewska, Alecia Neo, Alejandro Cartagena,
Ang Song Nian, Benita Högenbarth, Chadwick & Spector, Daniel Kukla, Daniel Stier,
Dave Wyatt, Eric White, Erica Lai, Frankie Callaghan, Gabriel Jones, Grace Kim,
Gulshad Kahn, Hyuk Jun Yi, Hyunmin Ryu, Ian Collis, Jan Leivisti, Jason Reblando,
Jenny Nordquist, Jo Ann Walters, Johannes P Christo, Kris Vervaeke, Kurt Tong,
Lek Kiatsirikajorn, Li Wei, Lydia Panas, Madhuban Mitra & Manas Bhattacharya,
Markel Redondo, Mika Whelan, Niall O'Brien, Paloni Mohan, Peikwen Cheng,
Phyu Mon, Pinapa Suthathongthai, Renzo Heilmanic, Samantha Tio, Sameer Tawde,
Sanjeev Thakur, Simon Carruthers, Simon Cuthbert, Subi Le, Tristan Cai, Tzu Cheng Liu,
Vincent Lim, Zhao Renhui

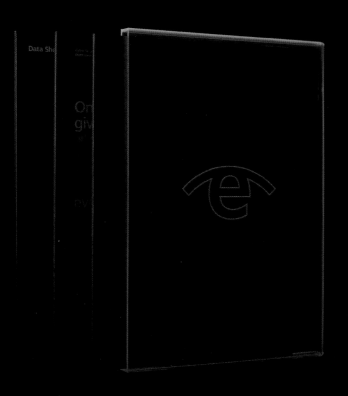

ENDACE BRAND IDENTITY

>■■ Endace specialises in high performance network monitoring and analysis. Preparing to take its business to the next level, Everything Design revamped its brand by visualising its promise "The Power to See All" with a new mark and marketing communications. Particularly produced for their initial dealings with foreign companies was a set of sales brochure, data sheets and brand book held in a transparent orange acrylic slipcase. A vacuum-packed set of lazer-cut acrylic tree decorations were send out as Christmas gifts to correspond the corporate literature suite. ■■◄

◉ *Design: Everything Design // Client: Endace*

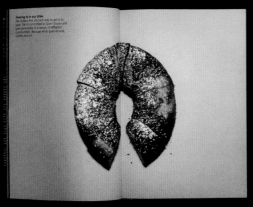

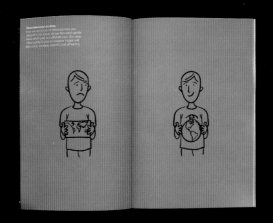

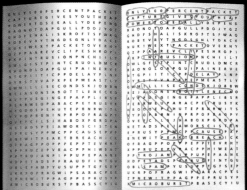

HOMAGE TO AESOP

▶▬ Aesop has been actively engaging with the cultural landscape, most evident in their character retail store designs realised in hands with designers and architects from around the world. Consisting 54 folded pages with artistic illustrations to reveal on the inner side, the corporate book contains stories and photographs from Corbis, to illustrate a romantic revival related to the brand. The brand book was designed with a violet theme and pages elegantly stitched bound and secured by riband. ▬◀

◉ *Design: Lloyd & Associates GmbH // Client: Corbis*

R ESEL
F PROBE

en Esel kaufen und machte mit dessen Beutzer

en Hof kam, wo schon mehrere andere Esel teils
eine Pro   der Fütterung waren, ließ er ihn frei herumlaufen

Als er mi   zu dem Faulsten und Gefräßigsten unter ihnen
bei der A   die Futterkrippe. Da legte ihm der Mann den
Sogleich tra   und brachte ihn dem bisherigen Beutzer zurück.
und stellte si
Strick wieder

"So schnell kam   chen und erfahren habe," wunderte sich der.
"Oh, mir genügt   ein übler Bursche!"
die er sich ausge

20/21   Kategorie: Ge
Lehre: Fre
einiges üb

 # SELF PROMOTION

▶■ Pop-up typography, innovative folds, foiling, special prints and stocks were the key in Hawaii Design's Self Promotion design. The set demonstrates the unit's passion and excellence in design and production in a unique mail-out, housing three bespoke posters, including a unique heat sensitive paper sourced from Japan and a pop-up poster beautifully foiled on Colourplan. All the posters were hand-delivered in a black gloss envelope to selected companies as to increase the studio's profile in the industry. ■■◀

◉ *Design: Hawaii Design*

167

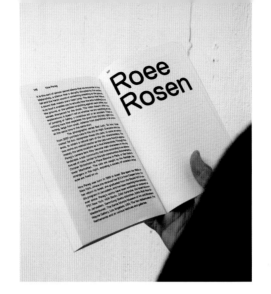

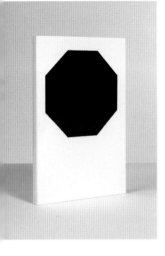

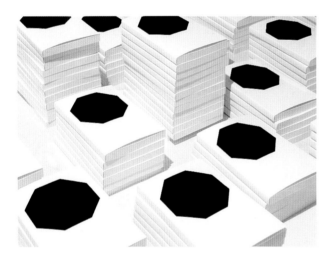

 # STOP MAKING SENSE

The issue of complex cultural identities, artistic legacy and socio-political orientations had been engaging artists that were based in but not indigenous to Israel. Having nine of them to present their unique approach to their backgrounds and identity, Stop Making Sense drew attention to what it meant for them to work and live in a territory that fell in the middle of "the West" and "the East". A stop sign completely painted in black and a background in contrasting white corresponded the nature of expressions as well as title – Stop Making Sense. ■■◄

⊙ *Design: Research and Development // Client: Oslo Fine Art Society*

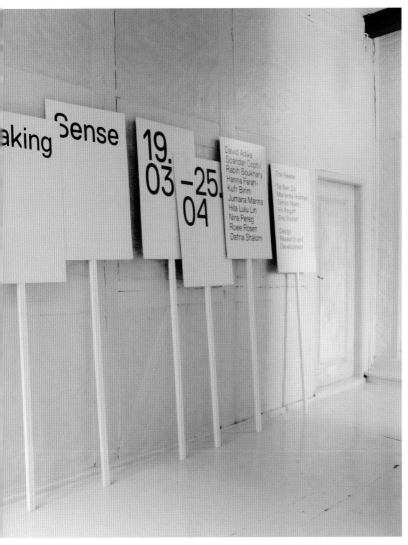

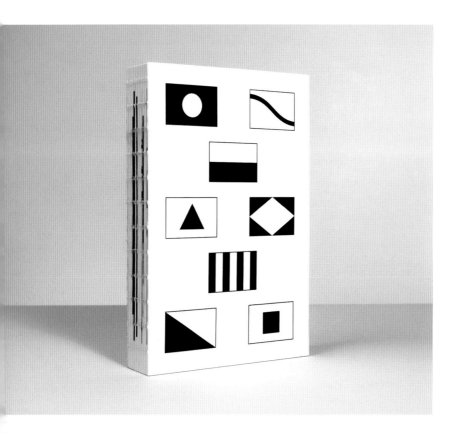

FAVOURED NATIONS

■◗■ Momentum, the Nordic Biennial of Contemporary Art is the largest visual art event in Scandinavia. Its 5th edition, comprising works by artists from Denmark, Finland, Iceland, Norway, Sweden, was titled "Favoured Nations", a term borrowed from international trade agreements. To the curators, the term was also a springboard for highlighting issues around equality, access and how people involved in artistic production were treated. With every indefinite thing removed, remaining was a spectrum of pure graphics extracted from national flags from around the world. ■■◣

◉ *Design: Research and Development // Client: Momentum, the Nordic Biennial of Contemporary Art*

Momentum,
the North, Moss,
Art and the World

Dag Aak Sveinar
Director

page 7

Notes on
unpaid labour

Angela McRobbie

page 247

Favoured Nations

Stina Högkvist
Lina Džuverović

page 199

Jani Ruscica

page 169

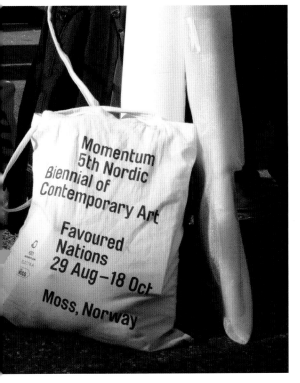

Momentum
5th Nordic
Biennial of
Contemporary Art

Favoured
Nations
29 Aug–18 Oct

Moss, Norway

Momentum
5.nordiske
samtidskunst
Favoured Nation
29.aug–1

Moss, 200

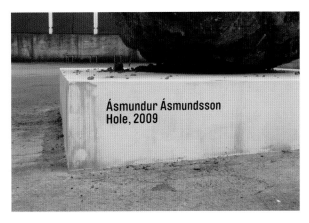

Ásmundur Ásmundsson
Hole, 2009

 # LETTERA 22

Olivetti Lettera 22 was a very popular portable mechanical typewriter manufactured by Italian manufacturer, Adriano Olivetti. The namesake promotional collection, produced for Plug-in Publishing, tells the human, industrial, cultural and architectural adventure of this great man. On the fiftieth anniversary of his death, a monogram '22' was developed and used across items, such as invitations, posters and pins to celebrate Olivetti's achievements during his lifetime. A part of the collection is now available at Adriano Olivetti Foundation. ■■K

⊙ *Design: ARTIVA DESIGN // Client: Plug_in edition*

TENOVERSIX
BRAND IDENTITY

▶▬◀ TenOverSix is Alice in Wonderland with a contemporary twist. Named after the price tag on Mad Hatter's hat that reads "In this style 10/6 (10 shillings and six pence)", the gallery-like accessories boutique took RoAndCo's idea, with inspirations from the vernacular of contemporary price tags, colour scheme of Monopoly money and gold "discount" stickers, for the brand image. The result was a simple, clean identity that could act as a neutral container for the ever-evolving boutique and concept space. ▬◀

◉ Design: RoAndCo, The Company & Collaborations of Roanne Adams //
Client: TenOverSix

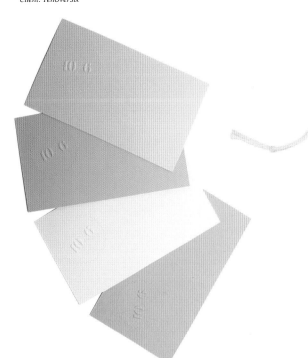

TENOVERSIX

CORDIALLY INVITES YOU TO OUR
PRIVATE LABEL FALL '09
PRESENTATION & COCKTAIL PARTY

DESIGNED BY
BRADY CUNNINGHAM & KRISTEN LEE
FRIDAY, MARCH 20TH 7-9PM

AT TENOVERSIX
7427 BEVERLY BLVD. LOS ANGELES, CA 90036
RSVP@TENOVER6.COM

10/6

TEN OVER SIX

7427 Beverly Blvd.
Los Angeles, CA 90036
tenover6.com

✦ PICCOLINA IDENTITY

➤▬ Every antique has a history. And, since there was too much to tell from every single piece introduced in the new Scandinavian vintage tableware store, Piccolina, COMMUNE decided on designing 14 icons, with each telling a different piece of Scandinavia's history or culture to the customers as they wander around the shop. As the icons collectively form the complete picture of the regions' important history, they also gather to represent Piccolina. ▬◀

◉ Design: COMMUNE // Client: Piccolina // Copywriting: Kosuke Ikehata

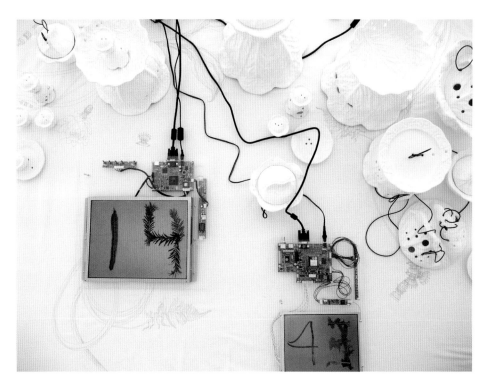

IMAGINERIES

 IMAGINAIRES embraces the fusion of figments and digitals. It is a collection of craft ceramics, glass domes and electric systems made to approach beauty and the way people absorb it, from the most singular details to surreal natural landscapes. For a refreshing display, the pieces were set to conjure up a new perspective of reality and surreal landscape with a network of interactive electronic device on display. Graphics were made to reference the installation on posters, windows and the exhibition environment to tell a story about craft and creativity. ■■◀

◉ Design: João Wilbert, Valentina Carretta, Catarina Carreiras / Fabrica // Client: ToolsGalerie, ICFF

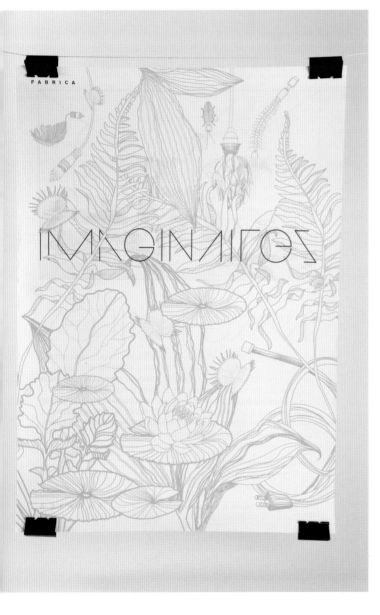

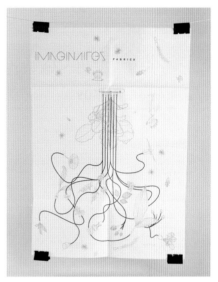

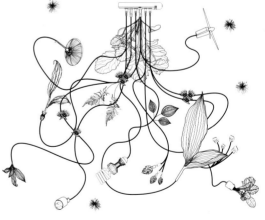

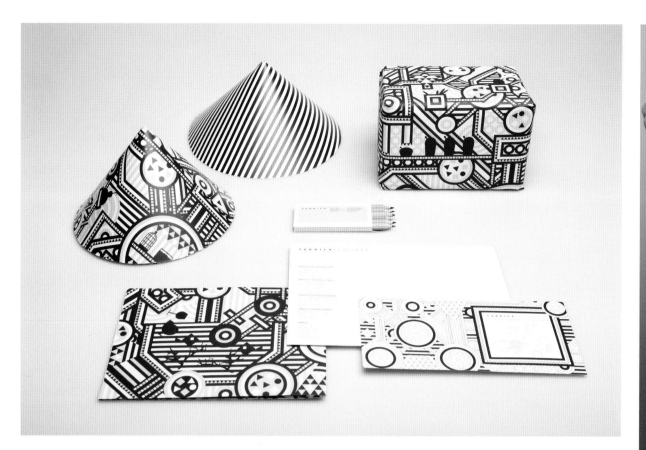

MERRY WISHMAS!

▶■ Wish away, keep on wishing, wish on, save a wish, build a wish, wish to wish, make a wish... WISH. Merry Wishmas! is Fabrica's Christmas campaign, stationery and display made for the research centre's three retail stores, Fabrica Features, in Lisbon, Bologna and Tunes. Every year Fabrica Features dresses its shops with an usual christmas feeling. An illustration was made using an imaginery Christmas factory as inspiration and later applied on postcards, posters, wrapping paper and display. ■◀

◉ *Design: Catarina Carreiras, Elliott Burford / Fabrica // Client: Fabrica Features*

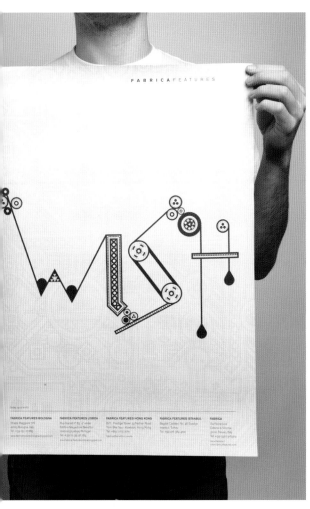

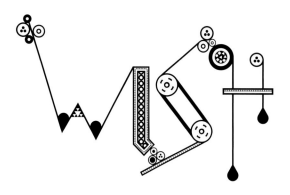

▐ TIMO WEILAND
❋ BRAND IDENTITY

▶■■ Timo Weiland is a two-man team based in New York who has been establishing their names with an edgy, antic quality in their men's and women's clothing design. Inspired by the brand's love of classic tailoring, unisex accessories and modern elegance, RoAndCo combined ideas of refined classicism, quirky details and contemporary street-style to create a uniquely "Timo" identity in black and white. The monochrome theme continued in Weiland's collateral and lookbooks. ■■◀

◉ Design: RoAndCo, The Company & Collaborations of Roanne Adams //
Client: Timo Weiland // Photography: Dan Lecca

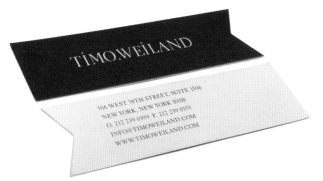

HONOR SPRING 2011
BRANDING & INVITATION

▶■ The invitation to Honor's first show for its latest women's luxury collection
was a mix of Parisian taste. Taking the chance to establish the Honor as a brand for
women who are as elegant and feminine as Catherine Deneuve yet wild and carefree
like Cyndie Lauper, RoAndCo pulled together fetish images inspired by French
New Wave movies, Le Ballon Rouge and Belle Du Jour, alongside a box of gourmet
macarons for the potential guests to taste. The result was a buzz in the fashion
community and a large turnout at the show. ■◀

⊙ Design: RoAndCo, The Company & Collaborations of Roanne Adams // Client: Honor //
Photography for Campaign & Collateral: KT Auleta

OPTICKS

Opticks was Arnsdorf's 2011 Spring collection, as well as the theme of RoAndCo's crystal design created as the collection's themed print. With the successful collaboration taking place, the revolutionary attempt of transferring "reflection, refractions, inflections, and colours of light" into a graphic crystal print was also extended to the invitation to the collection's debut and look "book". The diamond fold and pop-up concept in the collateral were consistent to the theme. ◼◼◣

◉ Design: RoAndCo, The Company & Collaborations of Roanne Adams // Client: Arnsdorf

BAG GOLDEN AGE OF COUTURE

▶■■ Organised by the V&A Museum in London, the exhibition explored one of the most glamorous and remarkable decades in fashion history. While the general public might not have a good knowledge of the designers or garments in subject, the promotional materials and identity were designed to evoke feelings of the glamour and style of the era. The hand-drawn dresses were a way of continuing the story of the identity, while the title composed of many light bulb-dots suggested the elegant charm. ■■◀

⊙ Design: Studio Round // Client: Bendigo Art Gallery

THE
GOLDEN
AGE OF
COUTURE

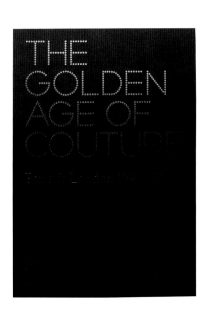

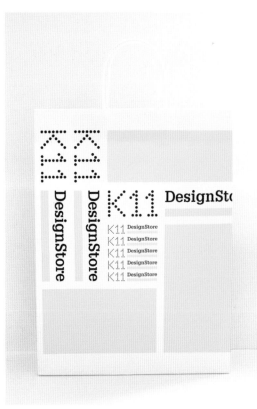

K11 DESIGN STORE
BRAND IDENTITY

▶■ Opened as a gathering place that integrates elements of art, culture and nature with shopping experiences, K11 Design Store is a young and inspiring retail outlet-cum-design museum where stocks sourced from around the world would be updated regularly on seasonal themes for constant surprises. An eccentric yellow was introduced as a neutral yet energetic background through its in-store collateral, environmental graphics and wrappers of the store. ■■◄

◉ *Design: BLOW // Client: K11 Design Store*

K11 DesignStore

K11 DesignStore

A destination where you could find
exquisitely thoughtful Christmas gift ideas

Merry Christmas!

K11 DESIGN STORE XMAS PRMOTION

▶■■ Having commenced business for just about a year, K11 Design Store and their offerings were still unfamiliar to local shoppers. For its first Christmas, a time for gift exchange and celebration, the store launched its first Christmas campaign and branded the entire space with a festive mood. Country flags, marking the origins of various stock, were applied in the catalogue and window display. A little snowflake was given out to customers as a special gift during the promotion period. ■■◀

◉ Design: BLOW // Client: K11 Design Store

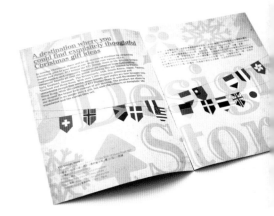

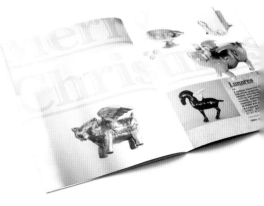

STATE OF THE OBVIOUS
— *A collection by* **MashCreative**™

STATE OF THE OBVIOUS

➤▬ Mash Creative believes there is a niche in the market for a collection of products which turns conventional branding on its head. State of the Obvious is a range of merchandise and apparel which do just that. As the name may suggest, the collection consists of branded items which "state the obvious". Fairly clean and simple in design, S/O/T/O uses the products description to create a unique brand identity. The collection currently consists of tote bags, notepads, mugs and T-shirts. ▬◀

◉ *Design: Mash Creative*

This is my
Mug Box.

This is my
Mug Box.

This is my
Mug Box.

This is my
Mug.

This is my
Eco-Frien
Reusab
Black
Bag

This is my
Medium

is my
ge

This is my
Degradable
Polythene
Postal Bag.™

This is my
Trusty
A5 Black
Notebook.

Fragile Item. Please Handle With Care.

This is my
Trusty
A5 Black
Notebook.

STATE OF THE OBVIOUS — A collection by MashCreative
— This is a 92 page, A5 Black Notebook. It can be used to write
or sketch almost anything and be taken almost anywhere.

STATE OF THE OBVIOUS — A collectio
— This is a 92 page, A5 Black Notebook. It
or sketch almost anything and be taken o

This is my
Eco-Frier
Reusable
Black Tote
Bag.

This is my
Eco-Friendly
Reusable
Black Tote
Bag.™

STATE OF THE OBVIOUS — A collection by MashCreative

— This is a 100% cotton Black Tote Bag. It has been lovingly screen printed with white ink. It can be used to hold almost anything and is much kinder to the environment than a plastic carrier bag.

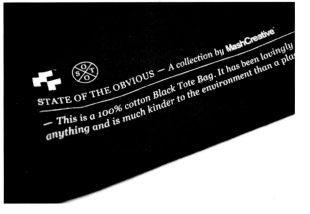

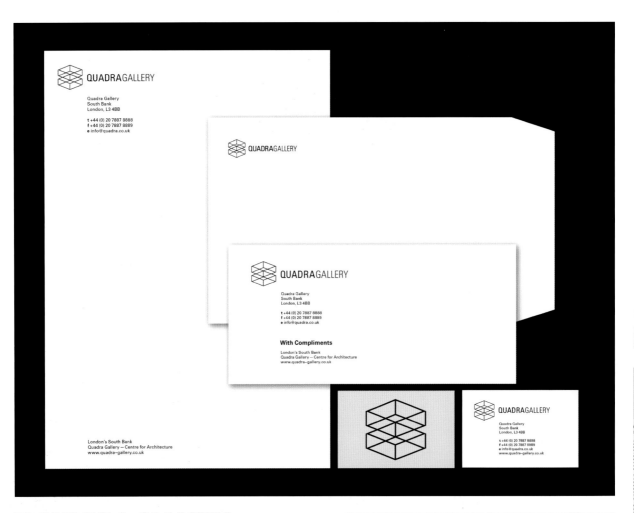

QUADRA GALLERY

'Quadra' is Latin for 'square'. For the visual identity and collaterals of Quadra Gallery, where developments of architecture were documented and displayed, Donna Wearmouth elaborated on her idea of how every architectural design began with a framework and created a set of structural characters to represent the gallery space. The framework system was expanded to graphically represent each featuring architects with reference to their signature style in design. This was a course assignment of Wearmouth, led by Mike Pinkney, while she studied at Northumbria University.

⊙ Design: Donna Wearmouth

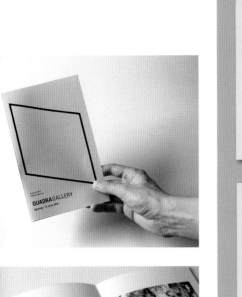

SKAGEN'S
MUSEUM
100 AAR

VISUAL IDENTITY FOR
THE 100TH ANNIVERSARY

▶■■ Founded to gather the works of the famous Skagen Painters, the Skagens Museum has been standing in the old garden of Brøndum's Hotel in Skagen for more than a hundred years. At the museum's 100th anniversary, in order to revitalise the glamour and glory of Danish art to the new generation, a new identity was introduced with red and gold for a new energy and classic athletics to replace the age-old stone-cut sign. The new identity was visible from the entrance throughout to its collateral for takeaway. ■◀

◉ Design: Designbolaget // Client: Skagens Museum

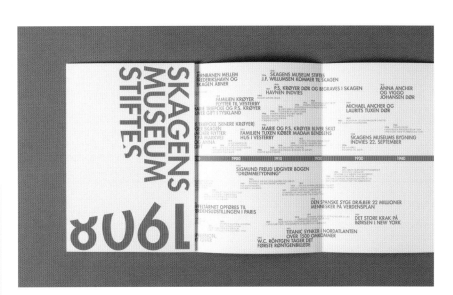

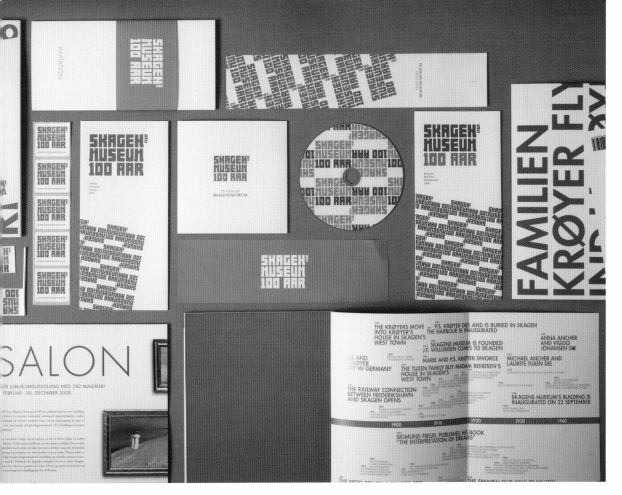

ERGONOMICS → REAL DESIGN

From the humble tape measure and the TV remote control to the vast and complex systems of transport and healthcare, ergonomics is the study of how we interact with the products, systems and the environment around us. Ergonomists gather detailed scientific data about us – the strength of a grip, the speed of a response, the capacity of our brains – and use it to design systems which are safe, efficient, and satisfying to use. Good design – real design – is centred on the user, involves the user in the design process, and creates solutions based on the user's needs.

www.realdesign.org

ERGONOMICS — REAL DESIGN

◗■ With focuses on the reason and science behind ergonomics, A2/SW/HK and exhibition architect Michael Marriot together devised a yellow-and-black scheme to tie in with the context of circulation and efficiency. A conscious effort to communicate the principles of ergonomics could also be found in a bespoke typeface named New Rail Alphabets, created in collaboration with Margaret Calvert. The thin line and arrow designs were extended further as applied graphics in the information display and communications. ■■◀

⊙ *Design: A2/SW/HK // Client: Design Museum London // Exhibition Design: Michael Marriot //*
Photography: A2/SW/HK, Luke Hayes

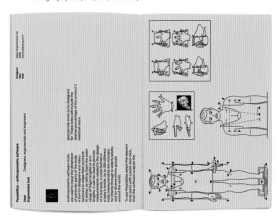

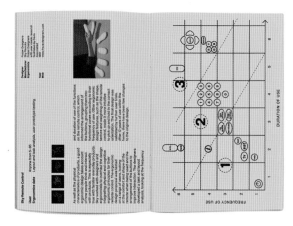

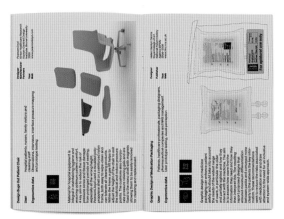

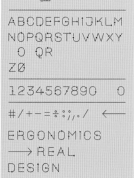

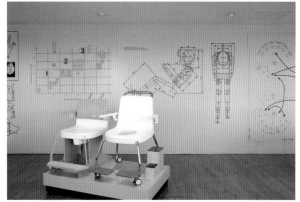

MUSIC EMOTION AGENCY

MUSIC E-MOTION AGENCY

▰◼ Music E-motion Agency is a Colombian music agency recently set up to nationally and internationally promote and market its resident DJs. It represents musicians and artists specialising in a range of music genres, including tech-house, minimal, techno and progressive house. The use of an in-house typeface combined with constructed shapes in surreal environment is integral in its visual identity approach. The art direction was simple but powerful in its visual impact and modularity. ◼◣

⊙ *Design: VBG // Client: Music E-Motion Agency, Colombia*

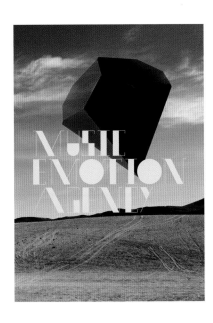

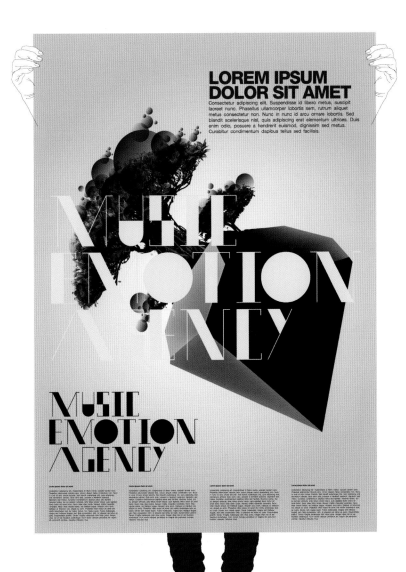

TRIPLEONE
S O M E R S E T

 TRIPLEONE SOMERSET

More than just a collection of exciting shops, TripleOne Somerset is a new destination dedicated to smart, worldly living. Emphasising on quality and design, its merchandise mix reflects a progressive, international perspective. The logotype, marketing brochure for potential tenants and hoarding for the mall were customised to reflect such diversity and dynamism as "new shades of retail experience" in its colour variations and dynamic types. The numeric logo cohered its motto and discerned itself from the rest within the vicinity. ◼◼◀

⊙ *Design: Asylum // Client: The Pacific Star Group*

PLANNING THIS EXHIBITION
para projectar a exposição

 # TAKE YOUR TIME

"Take Your Time" was an exhibition for the Fabrica Features as part of the program, Experimenta Design 2009: It's About Time, where Fabrica designers would attempt to analyse time by how it could be ruled by the objects and occurrence, other than using clocks, calendars and timers. Street posters were designed with a custom family of types and displayed in the exhibition with wallpaper glue, as a sort of contemporary manifesto on the way people are spending their time. ■■◤

◉ *Design: Catarina Carreiras / Fabrica // Client: Fabrica Features*

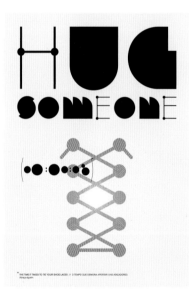

*OF DIRECT SUNLIGHT
de luz do sol directa

MEIN SCHIFF 2
NAMING CEREMONY
INVITATION

➤▬ Mein Schiff 2 was TUI Cruises' second biggest cruise ship. Its naming ceremony was to be attended by celebrities, business partners and the press. Looking to injecting something unique while preserving TUI Cruises' corporate blue, the invitation was a box of elements inspired by fashion rather than by the maritime world. The stylish notice was a composition of delicate details, including thick cotton cards with coloured edges, a little hand-folded paper ship and a silk scarf which guests could use to wave when the ship left the port. ▬▬◀

◉ *Design: Paperlux GmbH // Client: TUI Cruises, Hamburg // Photography: Michael Pfeiffer*

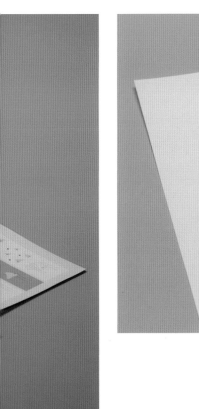

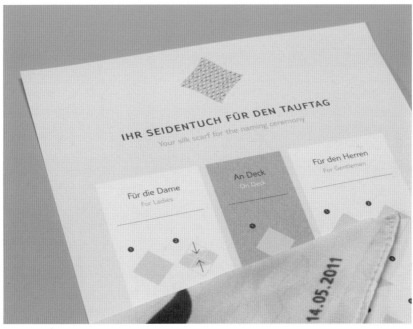

IHR SEIDENTUCH FÜR DEN TAUFTAG
Your silk scarf for the naming ceremony

Für die Dame
For Ladies

An Deck
On Deck

Für den Herren
For Gentlemen

14.05.2011

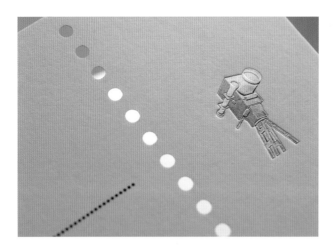

THE GOLDEN CAMERA
FROM HÖRZU

The Golden Camera is Germany's most prestigious design accolade for excellence in film and television making, organised by HÖRZU, a German television magazine. Considering only exquisite details could be a match for the awards which welcome talented stars and producers, handdrawn types and illustrations were applied on a textured 100% cotton paper wrapped in a very golden package. The design guided the whole after-show party, with the stay golden-motto visualised from ceiling to floor. ◼◼◀

Design: Paperlux GmbH // Client: Axel Springer AG, Germany // Photography: Michael Pfeiffer

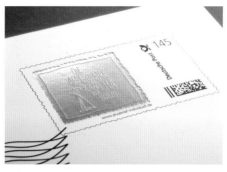

DARF ICH BITTEN?

ZUR VERLEIHUNG DER 46. GOLDENEN KAMERA
GEHE ICH NICHT OHNE DICH.

»DANKE!«

»IT'S GREAT HONOUR«

»WHAT BETTER IS THERE?«

DIE 46. GOLD KAMERA VON HÖRZU

IM NAMEN VON HÖRZU BITTEN WIR

ZUR DINNERPARTY ANLÄSSLICH DER
46. VERLEIHUNG DER GOLDENEN KAMERA DES
FILM- UND FERNSEHPREISES VON HÖRZU

SAMSTAG, 5. FEBRUAR 2011

AXEL-SPRINGER-PASSAGE
EINGANG ZIMMERSTRASSE 32
BERLIN-HALLE, BERLIN

IHR DINNERPARTY

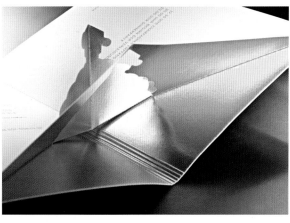

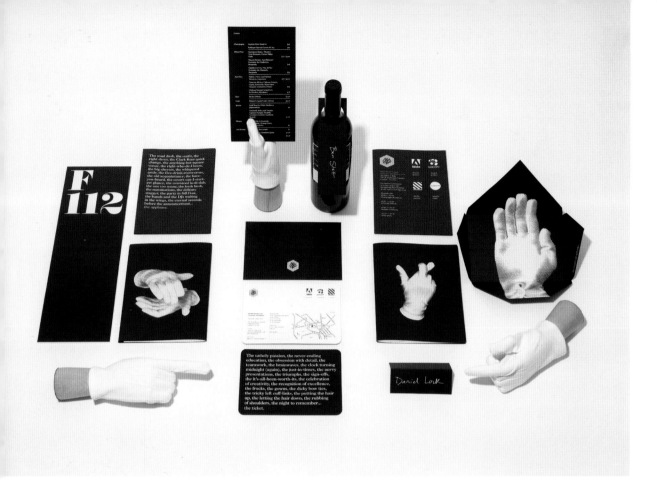

D&AD AWARDS CEREMONY 2009

▶■■ The D&AD Awards evening would be a very special night for creative thinkers after a year of obsession and breaking the mind-frame and, thus, the wit of magic was introduced to present the magical moments of winning a yellow pencil and values of the D&AD prize. The charisma and energy of a ringmaster were channeled through the white-gloved hands as a neutral extract of the MC responsible for animating the night, a conjuror, curator and the nervous, curious guests who made up the height of event. ■■◀

⊙ *Design: NB:Studio // Client: D&AD*

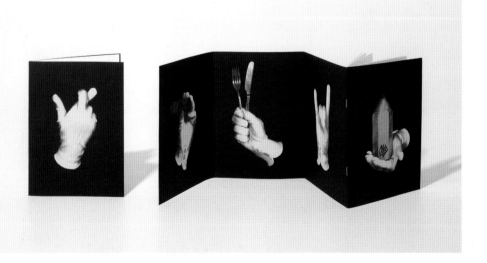

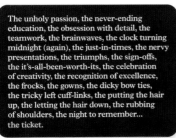

Level 1
Stairs

The welcome with open arms, the bar's over there, the back-of-calf shoe polish, the window reflection check, the pre-entry head flick, the shoulders back, the stomach in, the swagger, the butterflies, the tie-twiddle, the hair fiddle, the wall of noise, the friendly face, the oh-no-not-him, the seating plan, the smouldering glance, the night is young… The D&AD Awards 2009 Ceremony and Dinner.

The Very Important People

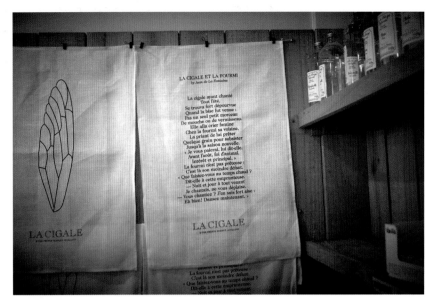

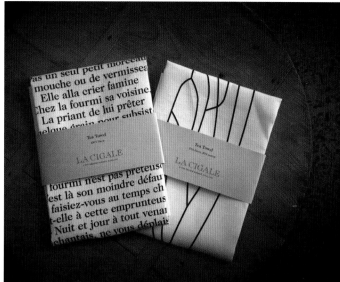

LA CIGALE
BRAND EXTENSION

➤■ La Cigale has most of its food and fashion products sourced from France. Hoping to make the brand more tangible for shoppers and diners, Everything Design developed a well-integrated visual identity system and a range of branded retail products to capture the market's eclectic French spirit and attention from shoppers and tourists who were on the look for a unique experience in town. On La Cigale's staff apron was a passenger list of whom embarked on the "Comte de Paris" bound for New Zealand in March 1840. ■■◀

◉ *Design: Everything Design // Client: La Cigale*

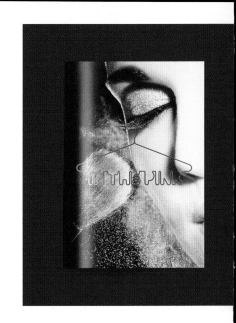

NZ BREAST CANCER FOUNDATION FUNDRAISING CAMPAIGNS

▶■ The New Zealand Breast Cancer Foundation is the country's foremost breast cancer education and awareness organisation. As a non-government funded charitable trust, the Foundation needs to consistently campaign for funds to support its initiatives. Aside from creating an integrated brand identity framework to ensure public awareness of the Foundation and their efforts, materials ranging from annual reports to promotional items for fundraising events were also produced with an urge for immediate action and support. ■◀

◉ *Design: Everything Design // Client: New Zealand Breast Cancer Foundation*

 SHIFT
– FRAMING A CITY IN
CONSTANT MOTION

►■■ Shift was a digital photography exhibition that captured the diversity of movement and travel on different corners of London. As briefed to
create a name along with a strong, graphic identity, Magpie Studio took
the word 'Shift' to allude to both "movements" and the type of lenses
used by the architectural photographers. Clear screenprinted posters as
invitations were sent out, with the central focus brackets offset to create
an iconic 'S', inviting recipients to frame their own view of the city. The
event was expecting a mix of designers and architects. ■■◄

◉ *Design: Magpie Studio // Client: Shift // Photography: Victoria Gibbs, Paul Grundy,
Murray Scott, Martin Stewart*

Murray Scott
On the Move

Clockwise from Left:

The remaining residents of the
Heygate Estate in Elephant & Castle
carry on with daily life as a wider
redevelopment occurs around them. The
estate will be completely demolished
and re-developed over the next
five years.

1st April 2009, G20 Day,
City of London.

Rush hour,
Waterloo.

The 2009 Serpentine Gallery Pavilion,
Kensington Gardens.

London wall.

Park Plaza hotel,
Westminster Bridge Road.

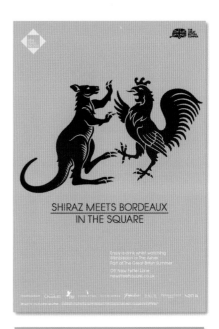

SHIRAZ MEETS BORDEAUX
IN THE SQUARE

MORNING MEETS NIGHT
IN THE SQUARE

RIOJA MEETS BORDEAUX
IN THE SQUARE

WHO WILL WIN THE ASHES?

NEW STREET SQUARE
ANIMAL CAMPAIGN

Land Securities is the UK's leading real estate investment trust. New Street Square, a shopping-and-lifestyle complex in London's mid-town, was one of their latest developments in town. As a prelude to the opening of the shopping plaza, the campaign used a series of fighting heraldic beasts to promote both the sports events and shopping choices to be available within the square itself. These animals were applied to posters, window graphics, website, direct mailers and an online interactive game. ■■◀

Design: Hat-trick design consultants limited // Client: Land Securities

MEETS SILENT NIGHT
N THE SQUARE

The Ashes 5 July — 24 August
Free live outdoor screenings
Part of The Great British Summer

Off New Fetter Lane
newstreetsquare.co.uk

G MEETS DARJEELING
N THE SQUARE

Caffè Vergnano
Moving in soon
newstreetsquare.co.uk

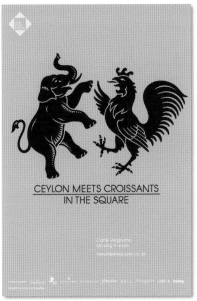

CEYLON MEETS CROISSANTS
IN THE SQUARE

Caffè Vergnano
Moving in soon
newstreetsquare.co.uk

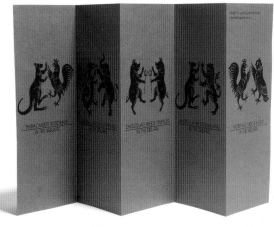

MURRAY MEETS NADAL
IN THE SQUARE

Wimbledon 22 June — 5 July
Free live outdoor screenings
Part of The Great British Summer

Off New Fetter Lane
newstreetsquare.co.uk

Brought to you by Land Securities

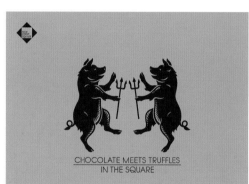

CHOCOLATE MEETS TRUFFLES
IN THE SQUARE

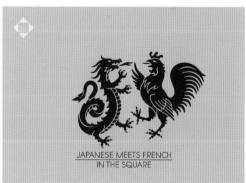

JAPANESE MEETS FRENCH
IN THE SQUARE

AUSTRALIA MEETS ENGLAND
IN THE SQUARE

AUSTRALIA MEETS ENGLAND
IN THE SQUARE

231

BARCELONA DIRECCIONS EXHIBITION & CAMPAIGN

➤■ Barcelona is a lively and crowded Spanish city. It is her asset and personality evident in her people, engines, ideas, environment and architecture. Commissioned by the Barcelona City Council who was planning on presenting the city's heritage, its vision and evolution in a cluster of re-purposed containers, clasebcn created a huge array of arrows, all pointing in the same direction but in various styles, to reflect a city that marches ever on. All the graphics were created with two basic colours to deliver the brightest, most optimistic Mediterranean message. ■◀

⊙ Design: clasebcn // Client: Barcelona City Council // Exhibition Architecture: Bopbaa

BIOGRAPHY

& SMITH

& SMITH is an independent graphic design studio based in London. Passionate about the craft and value of design, & SMITH works closely with clients to achieve a full understanding of the business, ensuring that the work they produce engages and inspires the audience. Their work encompasses corporate identity, branding, print, web solutions, book design, signage and packaging.

A+B STUDIO

A+B Studio was founded by Alex Lampe and Benji Wiedemann to deliver clear, relevant and innovative design solutions, which work seamlessly across multiple communication platforms.

A2/SW/HK

A2/SW/HK is an independent design studio based in London. Formed by Royal College of Art graduates Scott Williams and Henrik Kubel in 2000, A2/SW/HK works with leading national and international clients on design consultancy, art direction, branding, publishing, exhibitions, website design and bespoke typography.

AAD

Aad, short for Art and Design, believes that design is about crafting thought, idea and strategy while art represents the visual language for engagement and communication. The studio works for clients from international brands to small arts organisations. Rooted in graphic design, the team also produces work that touches on many disciplines including illustration, photography, fashion design, and interior & exhibition design. Aad does not have a 'house style', instead the team treats every project individually.

ALEX TROCHUT

Alex Trochut's illustrations, designs and typography take the modern notion of minimalism and flip it on its side. Trochut's work philosophy is "More is more". It is rich with elegant, brilliantly detailed executions that simultaneously convey indulgence and careful, restrained control.

ALEXANDER LIS

Currently based in Frankfurt Main, Germany, Alexander Lis is a graphic designer graduated in communication design at University of Applied Sciences Darmstadt. Since graduation, Lis has worked at different places, and has given talks and workshops at the Universities of Art and Design in Halle, Offenbach, Mainz and Darmstadt. He is also part of the self-initiated research project fourfivex.net.

ANGUS MACPHERSON

Angus MacPherson has graduated from Leeds College of Art with a First Class Degree in BA (Hons) Graphic Design. He is specially interested in typography and usually sees it as the centre-pin to his projects.

ARTIVA DESIGN

ARTIVA DESIGN is a creative studio located in Genoa, Italy, since 2003. Its work is based on the interest of two designers, Daniele De Batté and Davide Sossi, in visual art, graphics, illustration and multi-media.

ASYLUM

Asylum is defined as a creative company that comprises of a design studio, a retail store, a workshop and a record label. Since their inception in 1999, they have worked on cross disciplinary projects that includes interactive design, product development, environmental and interior design, packaging, apparel design, branding and graphic design.

B&W STUDIO

B&W Studio is a multi-disciplinary graphic design consultancy based in Leeds, England. Their commitment to creativity, combined with the forging of strong and lasting client relationships, define their approach that allows them to work in all areas of brand expression to create powerful and meaningful solutions.

BLOW

Established by one of the up-and-coming designers Ken Lo in 2010, who graduated from HKU SPACE Community College in Visual Communication and won the Champion of "Design Student of The Year", BLOW specialises in identity and branding, packaging, print, publications, environmental graphics and website design.

CATALOGUE

Catalogue is an independent graphic design studio specialising in design for print, branding, identity, books, exhibition and web. The studio was set up in 2010 by Tom Pratt and Oliver Shaw aiming to see every project from start to finish.

CATARINA CARREIRAS

Graduated in communication design from Faculdades de Belas Artes de Lisboa, Catarina Carreiras enjoys looking out for shapes, colours, places and ideas. She has been working with Sam Baron since 2008, first in Fabrica's design department and now as a consultant for Fabrica Features and Sam Baron & Co.

CLASEBCN

clasebcn is a graphic design and visual communication studio in Barcelona made up of a team of young, international, multi-disciplinary professionals whose work has won a number of awards. They work on all areas of design but pay particular attention to typeface and the element of surprise.

COLLECTIVE APPROACH

Collective Approach is a design consultancy specialising in branding, graphic design, art direction and online. Their approach is ideas led, and to help creating visually exciting and relevant solutions to every project. With a strong emphasis on details and craft, Collective Approach creates original pieces of work which stand the test of time.

COMMANDO GROUP AS

Commando Group AS is specialising in graphic design and illustration with a strong belief that all design is strategic. They aim to merge their skills and knowledge into solutions that aid products and companies be visible and to reach the target audience.

· · · Page 072-073 · · ·

COMMUNE

COMMUNE is a creative team based in Sapporo, Japan specialising in graphic design. Motivated by the will to make things better, the team works to encourage people and the society for a change. At times, their creations take people by surprise, awake their emotions, or even move them to tears. That is exactly what the team is looking to create and appreciates.

· · · Page 118-121, 176-177 · · ·

DEMIAN CONRAD DESIGN

Founded in 2007, the multi-disciplinary studio works mainly in the cultural field and the leisure industry, lending its expertise to everything related to events communication and visual identity. Based in Lausanne and Bellinzona, DEMIAN CONRAD DESIGN is always keen to work with clients who share the same values and objectives so that clients can play a full role in the creative process.

· · · Page 024, 060-061, 070, 132-133 · · ·

DESIGNBOLAGET

Owned and led by graphic designer and art director Claus Due, Designbolaget is an award-winning design studio located in Copenhagen. The primary fields of work are within the areas of art, fashion and music. Among other awards Designbolaget was named "Design agency of the year 2010" by Denmarks prestigious Creative Circle.

· · · 034-037, 056-057, 202-203 · · ·

DHNN (DESIGN HAS NO NAME)

DHNN (design has no name) is an independent visual communication studio established by Lucas Davison and Juan Crescimone in Buenos Aires, Argentina in 2007. The studio develops efficient communication systems based on strategic and efficient investigation and research on new alternatives. Their work ranges from research and strategic planning to branding and visual identity, interactive design, websites, and animation.

· · · Page 126-129 · · ·

DONNA WEARMOUTH

Donna Wearmouth is a recent graduate of Northumbria University's School of Design where she studied Graphic Design. She has achieved membership of the prestigious International Society of Typographic Designers (ISTD). After graduation, she has joined the design team at Gardiner Richardson.

· · · Page 200-201 · · ·

EVERYTHING DESIGN

Based in Auckland, New Zealand, Everything Design is a graphic design company working with a focus on effective communication supporting their clients' business objectives. The team has multi-disciplinary backgrounds and is always looking for opportunities to apply their skills in different areas of design.

· · · Page 041, 054, 080-081, 162-163, 222-225 · · ·

GOODMORNING TECHNOLOGY

Goodmorning Technology is a strategic design agency, which enables clients to strengthen their brand, services and products range to achieve business success through design and innovation.

· · · Page 092-093 · · ·

HAT-TRICK DESIGN CONSULTANTS LIMITED

Formed in 2001, Hat-trick Design is a London based multi-disciplinary design company working for a wide variety of clients.

Ranked No.3 in the Design Week creative survey, the team provides highest standard of creative design and project management with a collaborative, creative and strategic approach. Their passion is to produce work that achieves its targets by creating memorable, engaging ideas that are noticed and enjoyed.

· · · Page 228-231 · · ·

HAWAII DESIGN

Founded by Paul McAnelly in 2005, Hawaii Desgin offers a diverse range of skills within the creative sector. They are a new breed of studio that pride themselves in being more than a design agency.

Their clients range from luxurious brands in the retail sector. Hawaii Design is fast becoming a studio to watch and was nominated for Designer of the Year at the Design Museum London 2008.

· · · Page 166-167 · · ·

HELLO MONDAY

Hello Monday is a creative agency with offices in New York, Copenhagen, and Aarhus, specialising in creating visual universes across digital and analogue media. It is a visual identity-building, flash-revolutionising, talent-cultivating, image-moving, illustration-loving, campaign-developing, typography-polishing, fun-sharing, and idea-growing boutique "designery."

· · · Page 096-097 · · ·

ILOVEDUST

ilovedust is a multi-disciplinary design boutique specialising in creative solutions from graphic design and illustration to animation and trend prediction. They ply their trade in two contrasting studios located in East London and the south coast of England where the blend of two environments provides them a unique and inspiring perspective. The team collaborates with both in-house and global brands, working together to create fresh, innovative design that makes up an award-winning portfolio.

· · · Page 032-033, 075, 158-159 · · ·

JOHNSON BANKS

Run by Michael Johnson, johnson banks is specialised in building identity schemes for clients such as Science Museum and Parc de la Villette. Johnson has won numerous prestigious bits of wood and metal including eight pencils from D&AD. Dozens of his work is in the collection of V&A Museum. He also lectures on design worldwide and has written a book called Problem Solved.

· · · Page 066, 071 · · ·

KANELLA

First studied graphic design in Athens and later mastered in communication design at Central Saint Martins in London, Kanella Arapoglou mainly works for and collaborates with prestigious design agencies for the publishing and music industry. Currently Arapoglou is devoted to her own creative studio in Greece and teaching at the Technological Educational Institute in Athens.

· · · Page 046-049 · · ·

LLOYD & ASSOCIATES GMBH

Lloyd & Associates was initiated as an agency driven by intelligent resourcing, commercial creativity and exceptional branding experiences. The agency aims to develop products, commodities and environments within a coherent multi-disciplinary approach through experimental marketing, branding content and interactive communications.

· · · Page 164-165 · · ·

BIOGRAPHY

MAGPIE STUDIO

Magpie Studio provides strategic thought and clear market insight to an array of national and international clients by working with intelligent ideas that not only engage an audience, but also communicate a clear message. Their working approach is to listen to their clients, understand their audience, and solve their problems.

MARC&ANNA

MARC&ANNA is an independent graphic design consultancy founded by Marc Atkinson and Anna Ekelund in 2005. Work to help clients communicating their message clearly and intelligently with beautiful designs, the team provides strong and exciting ideas that deliver an end result beyond expectation.

MARK BROOKS GRAPHIK DESIGN

Working between New York and Barcelona, Mark Brooks is a graphic designer and art director working on a broad range of projects for diverse clients in both cities. Current projects include design for clients such as Nike, The New York Yankees, Lufhansa, SantaMonica, as well as a number of more self-indulgent personal design projects which he conveys graphic design, typography and visual communication.

MASH CREATIVE

An independent design studio based in East London, UK, Mash Creative works on creative projects that include identity and branding, print media and web design. The studio is always in search for alternative approaches, which is why their work is always unique, producing relevant and successful solutions that add value to their clients' brands.

MATTHEW HANCOCK

Matthew Hancock is a graphic designer based in London. He provides clean, high quality design for print and web, and is also a regular contributor to information design blog Information is Beautiful.

MELVILLE BRAND DESIGN

Melville Brand Design is a design bureau based in the "surf-city" Munich. Fascinated and inspired by the breath-taking powers of nature as found in rivers, oceans, mountains and forests, it was natural to lend its name from the author of the most symbolic of all untamed creatures that is said to have covered the seven oceans of this blue planet, Moby Dick. With Moby Dick, Herman Melville created one of the most remarkable stories in the World; thus inspired Melville Brand Design setting to create most remarkable pieces of print design.

MIKA NASH

After graduating from Ravensbourne College of Design & Communication with a degree in Fashion Textiles, Mika Nash worked as a freelance screen-printer for Zandra Rhodes. Nash and one of the other Ravensbourne graduates Gavin Insley set up their bespoke screen printing studio called Insley & Nash.

MIND DESIGN

Based in London, Mind Design is an independent graphic design studio founded by Holger Jacobs after graduating from the Royal College of Art in 1999. The studio specialises in the development of visual identities and has worked for a wide range of clients in different sectors.

MUTE

mute was founded in 2008 by Kenji Ito and Akahiro Umino, who both graduated from Kuwasawa Design School. Working to design things with original charm obediently, the team always look at the essence of what they work at, and believe by doing so, their design will fit in our daily life better.

NB:STUDIO

Established in 1997 by Alan Dye, Nick Finney and Ben Stott, NB:Studio is an awarding winning graphic design consultancy with a reputation for wit and clarity of communication based in London. They don't follow trends and their approach to design has enabled them to build strong relationships with clients including Knoll, Land Securities, Mothercare and the Tate.

NERVOUSWETHANDS

Graduated in Architecture with a First Class (Hons) degree at RomaTre University, Nervouswethands started work for his passion and went to Milan where he met people, had appetizers and attended a master degree in visual design at Scuola Politecnica di Design. The designer is currently working with Lola in Rome.

NOOKA INC.

Nooka is a New York fashion design company founded by artist/designer Matthew Waldman. Universal language is Nooka's ethos, which guides the creation of their products with enhanced functionality and a futurist philosophy. Nooka creates physical manifestations of ideas. Most prominently known for its line of time-pieces, Nooka has created a MindStyle™ brand, expanding their range to additional innovative accessories as well as a fragrance.

NOUS VOUS

Nous Vous is a group of artists collaborating on design projects, illustration, exhibitions and workshops. They have worked on a variety of projects, ranging from record sleeve design to creating installations for events. Alongside their commercial practice, the group frequently exhibits as an artist collective, creating responsive and self-initiated works.

OSCAR DIAZ STUDIO

Oscar Diaz is a product designer based in London where he works on self-initiated and commissioned projects for both cultural and commercial contexts. He studied fine art in Spain, and industrial design at École des Beaux-Arts de Bordeaux, before working for two years at Matali Crasset Studio in Paris. Diaz then joined the Royal College of Art Design Products department, where he graduated with an MA in 2006.

PAPERLUX GMBH

Based in Hamburg, Germany, Paperlux GmbH is a design studio with a staff of nine specialising in branding, corporate design, editorial design, event communication, typography, illustration, art, spatial communication, etc.

PLOTZ

Launched in 2007, PLOTZ has been pertaining to the spirit of communication between garments and human beings. Transcending to the ground of fashion, PLOTZ has made an impact on those standing in the forefront of style while sticking to their own characters.

Hinting to solidify the multiplicity of styles, PLOTZ stresses details from garment to garment. Innovative ideas and ambiguity are uncovered through collections. PLOTZ believes in the concept of fun harmony. A fan of comfort, PLOTZ jumps on the styling trend of basic colours with enlarged sophisticated details.

REKLAM2o1o, BECKMANS COLLEGE OF DESIGN

Reklam2010 is a class of 2010 in Advertising and Graphic Design at Beckmans College of Design. The class incudes Kalle Hagman, Petter Prinz, Andreas Lewandowski, Martin Wägnert, John Falk Rodén, Samuel Nilsson and Linn Mork.

Beckmans College of Design is a relatively small school with about 130 students who are divided into three courses, advertising and graphic design, product design and fashion design where the courses are crossed with each other. Located in central Stockholm, it is the only school of its kind in Sweden.

RESEARCH AND DEVELOPMENT

Research and Development collaborates with artists, curators, critics, collectors, directors, museums and cultural institutions. They design various kinds of printed works and occasionally arrange film screenings and produce or participate in exhibitions.

ROANDCO, THE COMPANY & COLLABORATIONS OF ROANNE ADAMS

Led by award-winning creative director Roanne Adams, RoAndCo, The Company & Collaborations of Roanne Adams is a multi-disciplinary design studio devoted to holistic branding that serves a range of fashion, art, and lifestyle clients, offering design, image, and branding capabilities across a variety of mediums from print to moving image.

ROB SCHELLENBERG

Rob Schellenberg is an art director and designer based in Chicago specialising in print and multimedia projects. He graduated from Iowa State University in 2009 with a BFA in graphic design. In 2008 Schellenberg served as an apprentice to fellow Chicago graphic designer Rick Valicenti at Thirst. He continues to lead creative endeavors on a freelance basis, collaborating with an array of clients on everything from identity development to packaging, environmental and interactive design.

RUIZ+COMPANY

Led by David Ruiz, ruiz+company is a team of professionals who are specialised in creating innovative brand concepts and codes. The team works in corporate identity, advertising, packaging and broadcast design. The team has been honoured with more than 100 national and international awards.

SAMANTHA ZIINO

Samantha Ziino is a young graphic designer from Melbourne, Australia. She graduated with a First Class (Hons) in Communication Design at Royal Melbourne Institute of Technology (RMIT). Her work has been showcased internationally, and has won numerous awards within the design industry.

SEBASTIEN LORDEZ

Sebastien Lordez is a young French graphic designer based in Lille who runs his own studio after graduating from the Fine Arts School in 2007. He has worked mainly with cultural clients from museums to music bands. The designer aims to give honest and thoughtful responses to his client requests.

SEESAW DESIGN

Named as what the studio ethos, Seesaw Design balances creative insights with company objectives to generate leading design solutions, with a little fun in between. Established in 2004, Seesaw Design understands the impact of brand and design on business. The team believes that design is a valuable commodity and creates with long-term intent.

SMEL

Founded in 2001 by Edgar Smaling and Carlo Elias, Smel for Smel creative and strategic design studio consists of a dynamic team of dedicated, multi-disciplinary creative people, specialising in strategic corporate identities, magazines, books, corporate identities, websites, as well as illustrious design concepts which subtly unite quality and imagination. It is an open-to-ideas company renowned for its high-end graphic design.

STUDIO LIN

Studio Lin is founded by Alex Lin who desires to explore new territory through challenging collaborations with creative visionaries in the fields of architecture, industrial design, art and fashion. After receiving an MFA in graphic design from Yale University, Lin spent six years at the design firm 2x4 and three years as a partner at Default. His work has been featured in leading design publications and exhibited at the Cooper Hewitt National Design Museum. In 2005, Lin's "Mies Face" mural for IIT became part of MoMA's permanent collection.

www.alexlin.org
www.defaultwebsite.info

STUDIO ROUND

Studio Round is a design company working across a variety of mediums including books, exhibition spaces, magazines, billboards, signage, branded three-dimensional environments, catalogues, brochures, media kits, websites, packaging, visual merchandising and a wide range of products. The studio draws on local and international experience serving clients including national government institutions, individual artists etc. and they love what they do.

STUDIOMAKGILL

StudioMakgill is an independent design studio focusing on the creation of brand identities and visual communication for a broad and discerning clientele. Their philosophy is to create succinct, innovative, beautiful solutions.

BIOGRAPHY

SUSANNE DUNKEL

German designer Susanne Dunkel has finished her diploma in graphic design in 2008. She studied at the Trier University of Applied Sciences in Germany and received a five-month scholarship from the Luzern School of Art and Design in Switzerland.

Dunkel is a freelance designer based in Cologne, Germany. She has worked with a range of projects including art direction, corporate identity, commercial campaigns, and arts and cultural exhibitions. Her work has been featured in a variety of magazines, books, design publications as well as a variety of design blogs.

THREE & CO.

Three & Co. is a Japan-based studio established in 2004, made up of a team of twelve professionals. Their business includes planning, design, creating, photoshooting, image synthesis and retouching for graphic advertisement, catalogue and web pages.

TOKYO PISTOL CO., LTD.

Established by editor Yohei Kusanagi and designer Kensaku Kato in 2006, TOKYO PISTOL CO., LTD. is specialised in graphic design, editorial design, and web design. The studio also produces their own company products such as the 'Bungo goods series'.

TOUCH BRANDING

Touch Branding creates compelling idea-driven visual identities and communication for brands on corporate and product level. From initial strategy to world-class standard execution through all appropriate touch-points, the agency works on both a long-term brand stewardship basis and individual projects.

TURNSTYLE

Turnstyle is a graphic design and branding firm founded on the belief that in a crowded marketplace, people gravitate emotionally toward companies and products that project a distinctive style. Their attitude is a correspondent to the words of French poet Jean Cocteau, "Style is a simple way of saying complex things."

UNDERLINE STUDIO

Based in Toronto, Underline Studio is internationally recognised for creating intelligent and engaging design solutions for clients such as Dyson Canada, Harry Rosen, the University of Toronto, and many more. Their work is classic and sophisticated. They have won Golds from the Advertising and Design Club of Canada, Graphis and the National Magazine Awards, as well as citations from the New York Art Directors Club, the New York Type Directors Club, Creative Review, etc.

VBG

VBG, short for Visual Brain Gravity, is a small design and development studio managed by the Žakelj brothers. Expert in producing and developing concepts, products and brand experiences, they tend to break the rules, not just in design but also in their thinking.

WATARU YOSHIDA

Born in Tokyo, Japan in 1987, Wataru Yoshida studied graphic design and illustration at Tama Art University. His work has been incorporated into different design mediums such as catalogues, posters, advertising, photography, T-shirts and manufactured goods. Yoshida was a finalist in the Adobe Design Achievement Awards in 2010 and 2011.

ZOO STUDIO S.L.

Based in Barcelona formed by four professionals with distinct backgrounds including graphic design, multi-media design, music production and video, Zoo Studio works to communicate well with clients and creates a good dose of self-criticism that allows them to reach the maximum quality. The multi-disciplinary design team believes that good design is the right equilibrium among aesthetics, functionality, innovation, technique and simplicity.

ACKNOWLEDGEMENT

We would like to thank all the designers and companies who have involved
in the production of this book. This project would not have been accomplished without their significant contribution to the compilation of this
book. We would also like to express our gratitude to all the producers for
their invaluable opinions and assistance throughout this entire project. The
successful completion also owes a great deal to many professionals in the
creative industry who have given us precious insights and comments. And to
the many others whose names are not credited but have made specific input
in this book, we thank you for your continuous support the whole time.

FUTURE EDITIONS

If you wish to participate in future viction:ary projects and publications,
please send us your website or portfolio at submit@victionary.com